Effective Family Engagement Policies

Aligned with the National Association for the Education of Young Children's Principles of Effective Family Engagement, this book helps early childhood administrators create effective family engagement policies that work. For each of the six key principles, this accessible guide walks leaders through the process of creating effective policy to engage families in their program. Filled with workable documents and templates to thoroughly scaffold the entire process, administrators will finish the work ready to implement the policies created, or build a plan tailored to their specific program. Designed for schools discouraged by the lack of engagement with all families, this book helps leaders strengthen the bond among home, school, and community.

Teresa S. McKay is Adjunct Faculty for Rasmussen University and University of Arizona Global Campus, and full-time Early Childhood Education Instructor at Penn Foster College, USA. Dr. McKay has owned and operated her own training and consulting business, Hands On Learning Early Childhood, since 1995.

Other Eye On Education Books Available From Routledge
(www.routledge.com/k-12)

**Trauma-Responsive Family Engagement in Early Childhood:
Practices for Equity and Resilience**
Julie Nicholson and Julie Kurtz

**Implementing Project Based Learning in Early Childhood:
Overcoming Misconceptions and Reaching Success**
Sara Lev, Amanda Clark, and Erin Starkey

**Advocacy for Early Childhood Educators: Speaking Up for Your Students,
Your Colleagues, and Yourself**
Colleen Schmit

**Grit, Resilience, and Motivation in Early Childhood:
Practical Takeaways for Teachers**
Lisa B. Fiore

**Trauma-Responsive Practices for Early Childhood Leaders:
Creating and Sustaining Healing Engaged Organizations**
Julie Nicholson, Julie Kurtz, Jen Leland, Lawanda Wesley, and Sarah Nadiv

**Nurturing Students' Character: Everyday Teaching Activities
for Social-Emotional Learning**
Jeffrey S. Kress and Maurice J. Elias

Effective Family Engagement Policies

A Guide for Early Childhood Administrators

Teresa S. McKay

NEW YORK AND LONDON

First published 2022
by Routledge
605 Third Avenue, New York, NY 10158

and by Routledge
2 Park Square, Milton Park, Abingdon, Oxon, OX14 4RN

Routledge is an imprint of the Taylor & Francis Group, an informa business

© 2022 Teresa S. McKay

The right of Teresa S. McKay to be identified as author of this work has been asserted by her in accordance with sections 77 and 78 of the Copyright, Designs and Patents Act 1988.

All rights reserved. No part of this book may be reprinted or reproduced or utilised in any form or by any electronic, mechanical, or other means, now known or hereafter invented, including photocopying and recording, or in any information storage or retrieval system, without permission in writing from the publishers.

Trademark notice: Product or corporate names may be trademarks or registered trademarks, and are used only for identification and explanation without intent to infringe.

Library of Congress Cataloging-in-Publication Data
A catalog record for this book has been requested

ISBN: 978-0-367-67911-8 (hbk)
ISBN: 978-0-367-67233-1 (pbk)
ISBN: 978-1-003-13335-3 (ebk)

DOI: 10.4324/9781003133353

Typeset in Optima
by Apex CoVantage, LLC

Contents

Illustrations vi
Acknowledgments vii

1. **Building the Foundation for Family Engagement Policy**   1
2. **Supporting the Foundation: The Principles of Family Engagement**   10
3. **Building a Comprehensive System for Family Engagement**   27
4. **Beginning With the End in Mind: Vision and Mission Statements**   44
5. **It All Starts With Relationships**   59
6. **Effective Communication Practices and Strategies**   70
7. **Extending Learning in the Home and Community**   83
8. **Decision Making and Goal Setting With Families**   98
9. **Decision Making and Goal Setting in the Program**   106
10. **Introducing and Implementing New Policies**   115

Appendix A   118
Appendix B   120
Appendix C   123
Appendix D   135
Appendix E   137
Appendix F   139

# Illustrations

Illustrations were created by Kathryn E. McKay.

Acknowledgments

First I want to thank my mentors, Dr. Ann Armstrong at Northcentral University and Mary Muhs at Rasmussen University, for believing in me and encouraging me to do more with this work. I want to thank the families and practitioners at Buttons and Bows and Discovery Time II for allowing me to do the research needed to really understand the topic. I want to also thank my family for their support and encouragement as well – they've sacrificed a lot during the writing of this book. My husband read through each chapter and provided an objective opinion and some much-needed clarification. Finally, I dedicate this work of heart to all the families I have had the pleasure to work with over the past four decades. Special thanks to the Hasselbring, Cooley, Crosier, Bean, and LaRocco families for sharing your children with me at Hands On Learning Preschool.

Building the Foundation for Family Engagement Policy

As with any structure, literal or figurative, it is essential to have a solid foundation on which to build. As stated by the National Association for the Education of Young Children (NAEYC, 2009), the family is the child's first and primary teacher. Given this, it only makes sense that the family is the foundation of the early childhood program. Everything the program provides should be based on the family as a whole – the service is paid for by them. Ultimately, the goal is to provide an educational program that fully supports Developmentally Appropriate Practice (DAP, NAEYC, 2009). However, the family must be wholly involved as a valuable member of the team.

Throughout this book, I will refer to those working in the Early Childhood Education (ECE) field with the children and families as *practitioners*. As the profession has grown, there has been debate on what we should be "called" – teachers, professionals, or childcare workers. "Practitioner" indicates what we do, which is to practice what we know is best for young children. As the field continues to create an image of professionalism, one of the most important aspects will be telling families what we do for them. By creating policies to outline the practitioner's role in service to the family, we define yet another piece of the professional hat we wear. When we further identify what is expected from the family, we communicate the need to be respected for our skills, abilities, and knowledge. *Family* and *families* refer to the child's custodial caregivers, because, as discussed in Chapter 3, no two families are alike. Often the extended family is tasked with assisting with the overall care and education of the child. The *community* refers to community members, such as those providing family support services and community volunteer groups and organizations. The community members will further be defined throughout the book.

In my four decades of work with young children and their families, one of the most vocalized issues (from both sides) was the disconnect between families and the practitioners working with their children. Neither families nor early childhood practitioners have been able to define what should be done to develop the relationships to support family engagement. The field is supported with documentation to guide best practices in providing services to families and to provide a foundation for ethically providing services to families but no foundational information on how to implement appropriate engagement practices that would benefit both the family and the practitioners in the field.

In 2009, NAEYC conducted a study about family engagement in conjunction with the *Pre [K] Now* movement on the foundational concepts for family engagement. Halgunseth, Peterson, Stark, and Moodie (2009) reviewed the work of three prior theories on family engagement to create an all-inclusive definition and framework for family engagement. When completed, NAEYC created the *Principles of Effective Family Engagement* (2010) as a foundation for engaging families. These foundational principles are summarized in the following list (NAEYC, 2010):

1. Families are invited to participate in educational decision making and goal setting for their child or children.
2. Families are engaged in two-way communication strategies.
3. Families and practitioners engage in reciprocal relationships.
4. Families are engaged through opportunities for learning in the home and in the community.
5. Families are invited to participate in program-level decision making and goal setting.
6. A comprehensive system of family engagement is created and implemented.

These are excellent guidelines for understanding what is needed to work with families, supported by research. What is missing is *how* these principles are applied and implemented. When practitioners look at this list, there is likely a feeling of "we already do all these things." However, there is a great misunderstanding of what each of these areas means and, more importantly, the real definition of family engagement.

What Does *Engagement* Mean?

Before practitioners can focus on how to build on these foundational concepts in their own program, it is imperative to understand the difference between family *involvement* and *engagement*. According to Goodall and Montgomery (2014), family involvement is loosely defined as the family's participation in activities, events, and situations created by the early childhood program. Involvement refers to defining the role of family members in conjunction with the program. In contrast, engagement includes creating the feeling of being an integral part of their child's educational journey. Engagement defines the role of not only the family members but the role of the practitioners and the community in forming reciprocal relationships – a partnership between the practitioners, families, and community members (Demircan & Erden, 2015; Hilado, Kallemeyn, & Phillips, 2013; LaRocque, Kleiman, & Darling, 2011). The differences in these two terms are further outlined in Figure 1.1 (McKay, 2019).

 Involvement

- Parents were considered free helpers, not equal partners.
- One-sided; generally initiated by the practitioners of the ECE program.
- Family members often felt guilty if not able to participate in the "events" of the program.
- Eventually, families "gave in" to the requests of the program's practitioners.

 Engagement

- **Relationships** are formed between practitioners and family members.
- Practitioners **actively seek input from the family** on how they want to or can be involved.
- **Practitioners work with family members** to determine a comfortable level and ability to engage in program areas.
- **Responsibility for the partnerships is equally divided** between family members, practitioners, and community members.
- **Strives to meet the family where they are**.

Figure 1.1 Involvement vs. Engagement

Clearly, the definition of engagement revolves around the concept introduced at the beginning of this chapter – the family as the primary foundation. When families are engaged in their child's education and the program they attend, everyone benefits. Family engagement is strongly supported and defined across the field of Early Childhood Education, as indicated in the following list. According to the U.S. Dept. of Health and Human Services, Administration for Children and Families, Children's Bureau (2016):

- Family engagement is the *systemic* inclusion of families in activities that *promote children's development, learning, and wellness. These systems and practices are used to enhance connections* between family members, educators, and community members.
- This means including families in the *planning, development, and assessment practices* of the program.
- Practitioners must *engage* families as *partners,* ensuring *positive relationships* are *nurtured* between family members, educators, and community members.
- *Family Engagement Practices are an indicator of QUALITY in a program.*

Subsequently, family engagement is a *critical and integral* part of quality care and *education policies* to support children's learning and development (QRIS, n.d.). The DAP position statement also indicates that family engagement is based on the knowledge of child development and the context in which each child is living (NAEYC, 2009). This knowledge is obtained by developing relationships with families.

Further, NAEYC identifies family engagement as a standard of professional practice. Practitioners are tasked with creating responsive and reciprocal partnerships with family members (Koralek, Nemeth, & Ramsey, 2019). NAEYC's position statement on equity supports consideration of equity and diversity of the working family and the need to respect the family as the child's first teacher and acknowledge each family's definition and understanding of their composition (Koralek et al., 2019). Practitioners can support these components by learning about each family's values, beliefs, language, and culture. Finally, practitioners must support the family's *right to make decisions* about their children's education, respecting the fact that these decisions may not coincide with professional knowledge.

In a meaningful partnership, both sides will find a mutual solution to any issues that arise. NAEYC advises programs seek accreditation to know and understand that these collaborative relationships should be established and maintained and assurance that families are encouraged to participate fully in the program (NAEYC, 2018). Finally, NAEYC has incorporated family engagement components to guide our practices in the Code of Ethical Conduct Core Values (2011). In general, practitioners have the responsibility to support the bond between child and family. The code also refers to the DAP statement in that practitioners use the context of each child's family, culture, community, and greater society to understand and support development.

In summary, an ECE program's policies and procedures should clearly define family engagement as a shared process by practitioners and family members to:

- Participate in a variety of program activities, and events promote and plan common goals for the development, learning, and wellness of children.
- Develop and maintain meaningful partnerships among the family, practitioners, and members of the community.
- Acknowledge and include the context in which each family is living, with respect for culture (values, beliefs, language), the family's definition, and understanding of their composition.
- Acknowledge the family's right to make and/or share in the process of making appropriate decisions for their child.

The question at hand, then, is: how do we implement these foundational concepts and truly engage families? Practitioners define policies and procedures for tuition rates, hours of operation, health, safety, and emergency procedures. There should also be clearly defined policies for how families are engaged in their child's education. Many programs have the "Open Door Policy," which defines that family members should have access to visit the program anytime care is being provided unannounced. While this is an important component of the policy, it does not define *how* you will engage the family. Suppose we look at the foundational concepts put forth by NAEYC and others for effective family engagement. In that case, we are left with the task of determining how to use them to build an effective policy. In this book, each component will be used as a building block to create not only policy but also examples of how they can be developed to meet your program's needs.

Building the Foundation

Why is policy important? Policies and procedures are *action* plans and provide a basis for accountability. Policies build a common language and describe, in this case, family engagement as something to be prioritized and used as an educational strategy. A policy defines what is expected of each member in the relationship. To build effective policies and procedures, the basic questions of *who, what, where, when,* and *why* must be addressed. For each building block discussed, you will be tasked with identifying the answer and procedures to implement each component. Remember the famous line from the movie *Field of Dreams*? "If you build it, they will come." This is likely what you are thinking: if I put all this effort into building this policy, will they engage?

The answer is not black and white, yes or no. There are never any guarantees. However, if you create a plan, some of the barriers that prevent good engagement can be addressed ahead of time. You will never reach/include all the people all the time. But for those you will, the relationships and outcomes will be richer and more successful for all involved.

Ultimately, the goal for creating and implementing an effective family engagement policy is to strengthen the bonds between home and program, family and educator, family and program, and families, program, and the community. As you work through this policy development workbook, use the building blocks image as a guide and understand that you will create *two*

Figure 1.2 ECE Field of Dreams

Kathryn E. McKay

Building the Foundation

policies – one for the family and one for practitioners. Each policy will work in tandem – the Family Policy will outline what will be expected of the family and what they can expect from the program. The second policy is for the expectations of performance by the practitioners. Now, where do we begin? What does your foundation look like? Write out some of your thoughts.

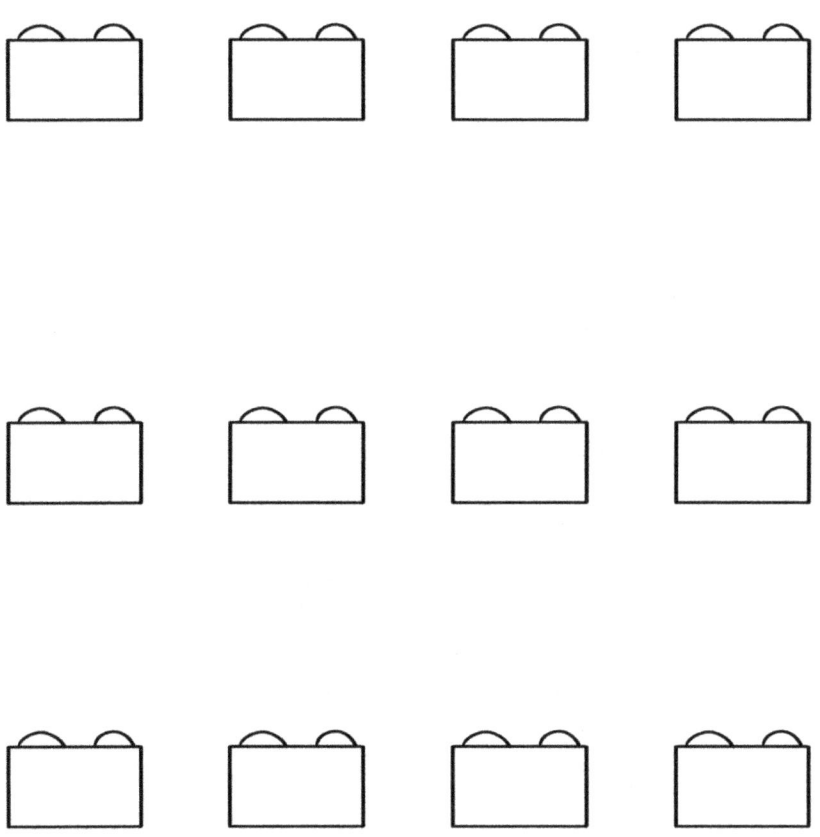

Figure 1.3 Comprehensive System of Family Engagement

References

Demircan, Ö., & Erden, F. T. (2015). Parental involvement and developmentally appropriate practices: A comparison of parent and teacher beliefs. *Early Child Development and Care, 185,* 209–225. https://doi.org/10.1080/03004430.2014.919493

Goodall, J., & Montgomery, C. (2014). Parental involvement to parental engagement: A continuum. *Educational Review, 66*, 399–410. https://doi.org/10.1080.00131911.2013.781576

Halgunseth, L. C., Peterson, A., Stark, D. R., & Moodie, S. (2009). *Family engagement, diverse families, and early childhood education programs: An integrated review of the literature.* Retrieved from https://nieer.org/wp-content/uploads/2011/09/EDF_Literature20Review.pdf

Hilado, A. V., Kallemeyn, L., & Phillips, L. (2013). Examining understandings of parent involvement in early childhood programs. *Early Childhood Research & Practice, 15*(2).

Koralek, D., Nemeth, K., & Ramsey, K. (2019). *Families and educators together: Building great relationships that support young children.* Washington, DC: NAEYC.

LaRocque, M., Kleiman, I., & Darling, S. M. (2011). Parental involvement: The missing link in school achievement. *Preventing School Failure, 55*(3), 115–122. https://doi.org/10.1080/10459880903472876

McKay, T. S. (2019). *A framework for developing diverse family engagement practices: A multiple case study.* San Diego, CA: Northcentral University. Retrieved ProQuest Dissertations from www.proquest.com/docview/2309682147

National Association for the Education of Young Children. (2009). *Developmentally appropriate practice in early childhood programs serving children from birth through age 8.* Retrieved from www.naeyc.org/sites/default/files/globally-shared/downloads/PDFs/resources/position-statements/PSDAP.pdf

National Association for the Education of Young Children. (2010). *Engaging diverse families project.* Retrieved from www.naeyc.org/familyengagement/about

National Association for the Education of Young Children. (2011). *Code of ethical conduct and statement of commitment.* Retrieved from www.naeyc.org/sites/default/files/globally-shared/downloads/PDFs/resources/position-statements/Ethics%20Position%20Statement2011_09202013update.pdf

National Association for the Education of Young Children. (2018). *Program portfolio tool: Early childhood program accreditation.* Retrieved from www.naeyc.org/sites/default/files/globally-shared/downloads/PDFs/accreditation/early-learning/program_portfolio_tool.pdf

QRIS. (n.d.). *Indicators of high-quality family engagement in QRIS and continuous quality improvement systems: Connecting research and practice* [Webinar]. Retrieved from https://qrisnetwork.org/member/calendar/event/190301/indicators-high-quality-family-engagement-qris-and-continuous-quality-0

U.S. Department of Health and Human Services, Department of Education. (2016). *Policy statement on family engagement: From the early years to the early grades*. Retrieved from www.acf.hhs.gov/ecd/family-engagement

 # Supporting the Foundation

The Principles of Family Engagement

In Chapter 1, the foundation for family engagement policy was formed through the many definitions of what it is and why it is essential. Chapter 2 will take a deeper dive into the foundation of NAEYC's (2010), principles. Before we can create policy, the foundation must be solidified, much like the mortar for bricks, with the understanding of how the principles came into being.

As NAEYC emphasizes throughout its statements, articles, and the Code of Ethical Conduct, the *family is the child's first teacher*. While we hear this statement often, what does this mean? In the 1980s and early 90s, we let the family handle family issues, and the practitioners dealt with the education issues. In other words, we told families they did not know the educational principles we were using to teach their children. In all honesty, back then, *we* (the field in general) did not even have a solid educational background. I had a Bachelor of Science in Elementary Education, but many only held high school diplomas or GEDs.

Additionally, in the late 1970s and early 80s, little foundational information about child development before the age of 6, let alone how to work with families, was provided in teacher preparation courses. We should have taken into consideration that the *family* knows more about their child than *anyone*! Who are we to think we can do this *without* them? Thus, we must engage the whole family – and how they define themselves – into relationships. The building of these relationships will be discussed in depth in Chapter 5. For now, let's take a more in-depth look at the NAEYC principles.

DOI:10.4324/9781003133353-2

NAEYC's Principles of Family Engagement

It is essential to look briefly into the history of parent involvement to understand how NAEYC developed the principles for family engagement. As indicated in the previous example, we viewed the home and the ECE program as two separate entities. Parent involvement was the passive participation in events and activities, creating a disconnect between the family and the practitioners working with their child (Barnes, Guin, Allen, & Jolly, 2016; Goodall & Montgomery, 2014; Morrison, Storey, & Zhang, 2015). One of the first recognized models of involvement, which included the following components, was developed by Epstein (2001) and had the following elements:

- Parenting – practitioners helping all families develop home environments to support learning.
- Communication – using effective formats to share programmatic and educational information between the program and family. In this model, effective forms included parent conferences, sharing work samples, newsletters, and phone conversations.
- Volunteer opportunities – active recruitment and organization of volunteers for various needs, such as clerical work, individual child support, field trips, and class parties.
- Support for earning at home – sending home activities related to classroom activities. These were generally in the form of monthly activity calendars and family projects for special occasions.
- Shared decision making – Epstein emphasized the importance of including the family in making decisions about their child's education. A subcomponent of this level of involvement was to develop the leadership roles of family members within the program and eventually within the community. Examples of this might include parent advisory boards or committees.
- Collaborating with the community – defined the family's role in the community as supported by the ECE program practitioners. The goal of community collaboration was to identify resources for families and to connect them to service opportunities.

Epstein's model indicated the primary purpose of involvement was to partner with the family in doing activities together rather than individually and sharing the responsibility of the child's development and learning. Epstein's work was implemented more as involvement, however, than actual engagement.

The Harvard Family Research Project (HFRP; Weiss, Caspe, & Lopez, 2006) further investigated supporting relationships among families, practitioners, and community members to create a network of complementary learning. The network created would be tasked with encouraging and supporting education and outcomes for children. Weiss et al. (2006) started with Epstein's model, condensing the components into three general areas using Bronfenbrenner's (1974) ecological systems theory as a base. As with Epstein's model, support for family involvement should be woven together in partnerships between family members and practitioners. The HFRP focused on the following:

- Parenting – this model's focus was to support the family members in nurturing and responsive parent/child relationships within the context of their cultural background, values, attitudes, and practices.
- Home–school relationships – referred to the formal and informal relationships between the family members and the program practitioners. Communication and participation strategies are the focus of this relationship, emphasizing *regular* contact between all parties.
- Responsibility for learning – primarily focused on the family's role in their child's language and literacy learning.

The HFRP study (Weiss et al., 2006) concluded that children's social competence, cognitive development, communication, and literacy skills were enhanced when practitioners applied these principles. This model's goal was to use multiple ways to approach involvement, both independently and through overlapping relationships. For example, practitioners promote and support the parenting role by providing educational workshops, thus reinforcing the home-program connection.

As with child development, family involvement should be a continuum. With that in mind, NAEYC and *Pre [K] Now* (Pew Charitable Trust Campaign, 2001–2011) implemented a study to define further a complete family engagement model, rather than passive involvement methods of the past. This model's focus was to include families' diverse qualities (Halgunseth, Petereson, Stark, & Moodie, 2009). Building upon Epstein's (2001) and the HFRP (Weiss et al., 2006) models as well as research from others, the Engaging Diverse Families Project (EDF, Halgunseth et al., 2009) was launched and is the foundation of the NAEYC's Principles of Effective Family Engagement. This study's focus was on quality, of which family engagement is a significant component. Halgunseth et al. (2009) started with the assumption that all families are, at a minimum, passively involved at some level with their child's well-being and learning. In this model, practitioners create high-quality, diverse family engagement practices that would include a) the development of reciprocal relationships defined by trust, shared values, b) ongoing and two-way communication, c) respect, and d) an identification of the needs of each member of the partnership. The principles are further described and defined in the following sections.

Decision Making and Goal Setting

The first principle for family engagement is including families in the decision-making and goal-setting process for their child (NAEYC, 2010). As indicated in Epstein's (2001) study, practitioners should actively welcome and invite families to share in the process of decision making as it concerns their child's education. Collaborative goal setting supports the child's learning at home, and families have a better understanding of the learning process (NAEYC, 2010). Additionally, because practitioners are the primary adults in a child's life *after* the family, there is a need for a collaborative relationship within the decision-making process (Alacam & Olgan, 2017; Hilado, Kallemeyn, Leow, Lundy, & Israel, 2011). The No Child Left Behind Act (NCLB) of 2002 indicated that the family should play an integral role in their child's learning process. Practitioners should encourage that role through active involvement in the program supporting the family as a full *partner* in the decision-making process. This partnership should include the *child* as well – they should be able to participate in their own learning goals and decisions from an early age. For example, a child could use drawings to express his/her learning. The child should explain work samples collected by practitioners during conferences. Children experience academic success *despite* existing adverse issues such as poverty or cultural background when the family is involved in this process.

In this principle, NAEYC (2010) uses the word "invite," which might throw some practitioners off guard. As I mentioned earlier, we often think that the "Open Door Policy" *is* an invitation, but, when we look deeper, are *decision making* and *goal setting* covered? Here is the "Open Door" policy from my program:

> Our center has an "open door" policy, which means we encourage your visits, participation, and comments at all times. No appointment is necessary to come in and visit with or observe your child, but we ask that you check in with the office or sign-in desk before going to your child's room. We have observation windows in every classroom, which allow you to observe your child without being seen. We do ask that if someone is coming to visit your child who is unfamiliar to us, a note must be sent in with the visitor's name, and the visitor has proper identification (picture ID). In cases where there is a custodial conflict between parents, we require legal documentation as to visitation rights.

Where is the invitation for families to engage, let alone help make decisions or set goals for their child? This statement only enables the family to know they are welcome to *visit*. An essential part of a comprehensive family engagement system is for *all members* to support the child's growth and development (Epstein, 2001; Halgunseth et al., 2009; NAEYC, 2010; Weiss et al., 2006). How might that support look? Practitioners should be providing families with information on developmental milestones and state Early Learning Standards to help families *understand the curriculum's goals*. The responsibility for these resources and activities lies not only with practitioners but also with the family (Halgunseth et al., 2009). For example, when families share their cultural background, values, beliefs, and traditions, practitioners learn how to better support children's education.

Through this type of support, family members will be more prepared to assist in their child's educational decisions and goals. The primary focus for family engagement is academic support and ensuring children are ready to succeed as they progress from early childhood to elementary school and beyond (Weiss et al., 2006). When decision making is a shared component, the child's goals and future activities are mutually agreed upon by all involved. Many practitioners may recognize this as a significant part of the Individual Education Plan (IEP) process – why wouldn't we do this for *all* children?

Children benefit from observing their family participate in this process. They will likely begin to understand the process of decision making through the sharing of different opinions, ideas, and views to achieve shared goals (Epstein, 2001). Families feel empowered in this process because their thoughts and beliefs are being heard and discussed. Even when results are not exactly what they had in mind – they have *ownership* in the process. Additionally, family members learn more about the rules and regulations that govern the early childhood program. Finally, practitioners will better understand family perspectives and use this information to build reciprocal relationships.

Of course, there are challenges to implementing sound policies and procedures for this principle, including time, money, language barriers, and the ability to include all families due to their diverse backgrounds (Epstein, 2001; Morrison et al., 2015). Often practitioners may lack the type of leadership skills needed to engage families at this level, indicating a need to provide training, which can be an additional cost to the program. You will work on this policy later in the book. These are examples of the specific issues you will need to identify as they relate to your current situation and plan for overcoming these barriers.

Two-Way Communication

Communication is likely the single most important component of working with families; however, we often struggle with it the most. The second principle for effective engagement is the concept of using two-way (the need for both program and family-initiated communication), collaborative communication (Epstein, 2001; Halgunseth et al., 2009; NAEYC, 2010; Weiss et al., 2006). Communication is an essential foundation in all relationships but especially important in the relationship between family and practitioners. We must build communication practices based on mutual trust and respect (Ma, Shen, Krenn, Hu, & Yuan, 2016; Nitecki, 2015). Effective communication practices must also be timely and continuous, focusing primarily on the child's education and the overall program policies and activities that include families (NAEYC, 2010; Smetzer-Anderson & Roessler, 2016). Epstein and Sheldon (2016) stated that effective communication practices are those in which all members *gain knowledge, exchange ideas, and develop a plan of action.* When communication strategies are robust, we create a collaborative system that supports the educational program, families, and healthier communities (Epstein & Sheldon, 2016; Garbacz, McDowall, Schaughency, Sheridan, & Welch, 2015; Goodall & Montgomery, 2014; Tran, 2014).

This process includes a collaborative exchange of knowledge between the family and practitioners, sharing each other's perspectives and learning about the child within the family culture and community context (Halgunseth et al., 2009; Mahmood, 2013). Like the mandate for shared decision making, the NCLB Act of 2001 (2002) suggested that practitioners develop a system of two-way communication regarding children's learning and the sharing of information related to the program, family development and support, culture, and community services (Morrison et al., 2015; Tran, 2014).

We must also "evolve" from only using one-way communication. In this scenario, practitioners are the primary communicators, sending notes, calling, sending newsletters, and sending daily activity sheets *to* the family. Two-way communication asks for communication *from* the family. Using various formats and *inviting* the family to provide information about them and the child, we begin to communicate collaboratively. Practitioners must ask how, when, and by what means they prefer to communicate and what information they want to know or share.

Reciprocal Relationships

Comprehensive, collaborative communication strategies are the foundation for developing relationships with families. Practitioners, children, and families benefit from sharing resources and information (NAEYC, 2010). Practitioners must actively seek out information about each family's life within the home and community context to understand each one's unique dynamic. The third principle of family engagement outlined by NAEYC (2010) focuses on the ideal family–practitioner relationships' reciprocal nature. In developing their position statement on DAP (NAEYC, 2010), NAEYC focused on creating reciprocal relationships with families, including the foundational component of respecting the family as the child's first and primary educator.

The definition of partnerships or relationships in family engagement refers to the way each member gets to know each other, establishes trust, and learns each other's needs. The partnership allows all members to work together for a mutual solution to goals set primarily for the benefit of the child and family (Knight-McKenna & Hollingsworth, 2016; McNeal, 2015; Share & Kerrins, 2013; Zhang, 2015). Thus, developing these relationships is equally divided among the members. All have equal power and control over decision-making processes.

Building relationships with families may not always be easy. Often practitioners mistakenly believe that families should defer to the practitioner's decisions regarding the child's educational (and program) needs (Whyte & Karabon, 2016). Practitioners may worry about offending family members with questions, feeling they are invading their private lives. However, engagement focuses on the family's and practitioner's *common interests* and investment in the child's well-being and education (Hilado et al., 2011; Murray, McFarland-Piazza, & Harrison, 2015; NAEYC, 2010; Winder & Corter, 2016). Shared interests and goals provide a starting point to develop relationships that, in turn, help with decision making and quality communication. Family members and practitioners bring their unique perspective and knowledge to the relationship, strengthening the nature of reciprocity (Winder & Corter, 2016). Think of building these relationships as similar to climbing a ladder – achieving one step at a time and understanding that it requires time and effort from everyone.

As in the decision-making process, it is essential to include the child in the reciprocal relationship process. There is support for child participation through theories such as Vygotsky's Zone of Proximal Development (ZPD), where children are both affected by and affect their interactions with adults. The ZPD is where the adult's guidance leads to the child's ultimate autonomy in learning and self-identity development (Ghiratto & Mazzoni, 2013). Together, family members and practitioners should encourage children to express their ideas and support them through their implementation.

Learning at Home and in the Community

When practitioners support reciprocal relationships with the families, they obtain information that will also help families provide educational experiences outside of the early childhood program (NAEYC, 2010). The fourth principle outlined by NAEYC (2010) emphasizes the need for the program practitioners to provide learning activities in the home and in the community. Home-based involvement includes those activities in which practitioners assist families outside of the program in promoting academic skills (Garbacz et al., 2015; Mendez, 2010; Murray et al., 2015). Providing high-quality at-home activities enhances the family's ability to support their child's education (Demircan & Erden, 2015; Halgunseth et al., 2009; Murray et al., 2015).

Learning at home begins with each family's belief that learning is essential (Calzada et al., 2015; Goodall & Montgomery, 2014; Hornby & Lafaele, 2011). While family members may be aware of this concept, they may lack the confidence to provide learning opportunities within the home (Calzada et al., 2015; Goodall & Montgomery, 2014). Practitioners should support family members in this endeavor by suggesting ways to establish an environment at home that supports learning and providing materials from the program that coincide with current curricular goals (Epstein, 2001; McWayne & Melzi, 2014).

ECE practitioners must look at how they can support the family in their role in children's lives. It is essential to understand when and how to deliver family education opportunities and learn how to actively incorporate volunteer experiences that fit family lifestyles in both the home and community. Practitioners must remember that the family is considered the child's first and primary teacher, and family members should be considered co-educators with program practitioners. The home is the first educational program children experience. The home–program connection is integral to the family engagement system, especially for low-income and minority families (Ihmeideh & Oliemat, 2015; Mendez, 2010; Schaub, 2015; Smith, 2014). As with other engagement components, the NCLB Act indicated that practitioners should support families in educating their children in the home (Morrison et al., 2015).

The benefits of bridging learning between home and school are numerous. The most important outcome for children is the continuous support for and development of skills and knowledge (Summer & Summer, 2014). The child also begins to develop a love for learning, a vital need for continued academic success (Epstein, 2001; Ihmeideh & Oliemat, 2015). Self-concept develops through this collaboration. Family members develop an appreciation and awareness of their child as capable learners (Epstein, 2001). Families benefit by learning how to support and encourage the children in their learning, as well as gaining an understanding of ECE best practices for curriculum and instruction. As part of the relationship aspect desired for families and practitioners, learning at home supports respect for family time and their ability to participate in the child's education (Epstein, 2001).

Learning support extends to the community, as well. Developing a collaborative relationship among community members requires all members to immerse themselves in the cultures represented. In turn, practitioner's family policies and practices of practitioners and the children's education and development grow stronger (Epstein, 2001; Sánchez & Walsh, 2017). Practitioners must actively identify and implement community resources and services to support families and children as part of the educational process (Hilado, Kallemeyn, & Phillips, 2013; Morrison et al., 2015). Such resources include programs that work with families in the areas of health, safety, financial education and support, diversity, and social support and that can link families to community activities (Erdener & Knoeppel, 2018; Epstein, 2001; Hilado et al., 2011; Weiss et al., 2006). Practitioners can further support families within the community by finding collaborative service opportunities that include children, family, and program representatives, such as a community garden or recycling project (Erdener & Knoeppel, 2018; Epstein, 2001).

Once family members feel they have support in their role, they are more inclined to formulate a partnership with practitioners and community members (Epstein, 2001). Practitioners also benefit by developing respect for family strengths and efforts in their role in the child's education and developing ongoing relationships with community services and agencies (Epstein, 2001; Hilado et al., 2011).

Creating a community collaboration system can be challenging in many ways, including finding the resources and services that meet the needs of the families (Epstein, 2001). One of the barriers to community support lies within the social status of the profession itself – the view of providing a babysitting service rather than a valuable part of the education system (Mahmood, 2013). Many community agencies may also be reluctant to enter collaborative relationships due to funding or available employee community service hours (Hornby & Lafaele, 2011).

Children, families, and practitioners benefit from community collaboration through access to extracurricular experiences that may not otherwise be available to them because of financial limitations or other constraints. Children become aware of the many career options and future educational experiences available to explore by observing and participating in collaborative relationships. Children learn to be participative community members as young children and how to access services for support (Epstein, 2001).

Program-Level Decision Making and Advocacy

The fifth area for family engagement policy in ECE programs includes involving families in program-level decision making and advocacy events (NAEYC, 2010). As relationships grow and develop, practitioners must invite families to participate in the program's governance, such as participating on an advisory board or representing families on the board of directors (NAEYC, 2010). As part of the leadership role, parents often become involved in advocacy for reform and improvement for the field and serve on family-oriented committees outside of the program where their children attend (Epstein, 2001). Practitioners should ask for family input on decisions concerning the whole program, especially those regarding policies and procedures that affect them directly (Epstein, 2001). To support families in this role, program practitioners should provide family members with the resources and materials to help them become informed advocates (Epstein, 2001; NAEYC, 2010; Sánchez & Walsh, 2017). Practitioners include families in advocating for services that are fair and responsive to family needs. It is essential to involve family members in the process, as they are the primary recipients of those services (Sánchez & Walsh, 2017).

The NCLB Act of 2002 and the Family Engagement Act of 2011 defined engagement as the shared responsibility between the family and education program for student success (Hilado et al., 2013; Morrison et al., 2015). The mandates also indicated the need for the educational program to work with community organizations to engage families in meaningful ways and for the family to be an active supporter of the child's learning and development (Hilado et al., 2013). High-quality family engagement occurs when program practitioners support families through validation of their participation as decision makers in their child's education (Hilado et al., 2013). Not only is the family considered to be the child's first teacher, but they also are her or his advocate (Brown, Knoche, Edwards, & Sheridan, 2009; Halgunseth et al., 2009). Families supported through various methods by practitioners feel more comfortable being involved in program decision making. High-quality programs involve families through parent advisory councils or topical committees such as curriculum, safety, or health and nutrition. Some families may even participate in advocacy groups to lobby for better child-development policies (Hilado et al., 2013). Regardless of how they become involved, networking begins, building stronger relationships.

Further, practitioners should encourage and develop family members into active leaders for the program and the community (Epstein, 2001).

The benefit for children when families are involved in a program's decision-making process is an understanding of their rights to be heard and supported. Families benefit from this type of involvement by having the ability to input thoughts and ideas into policies and procedures that affect their children. Additionally, there is a deepening of networking with other families and a feeling of ownership in their child's education. Families also learn about state and national regulatory policies and procedures.

Now that you understand the purpose of each principle, how can you apply this to your foundation created in Chapter 1? Create a block for each of the principles, then identify the core ideas you will want to address in your policy.

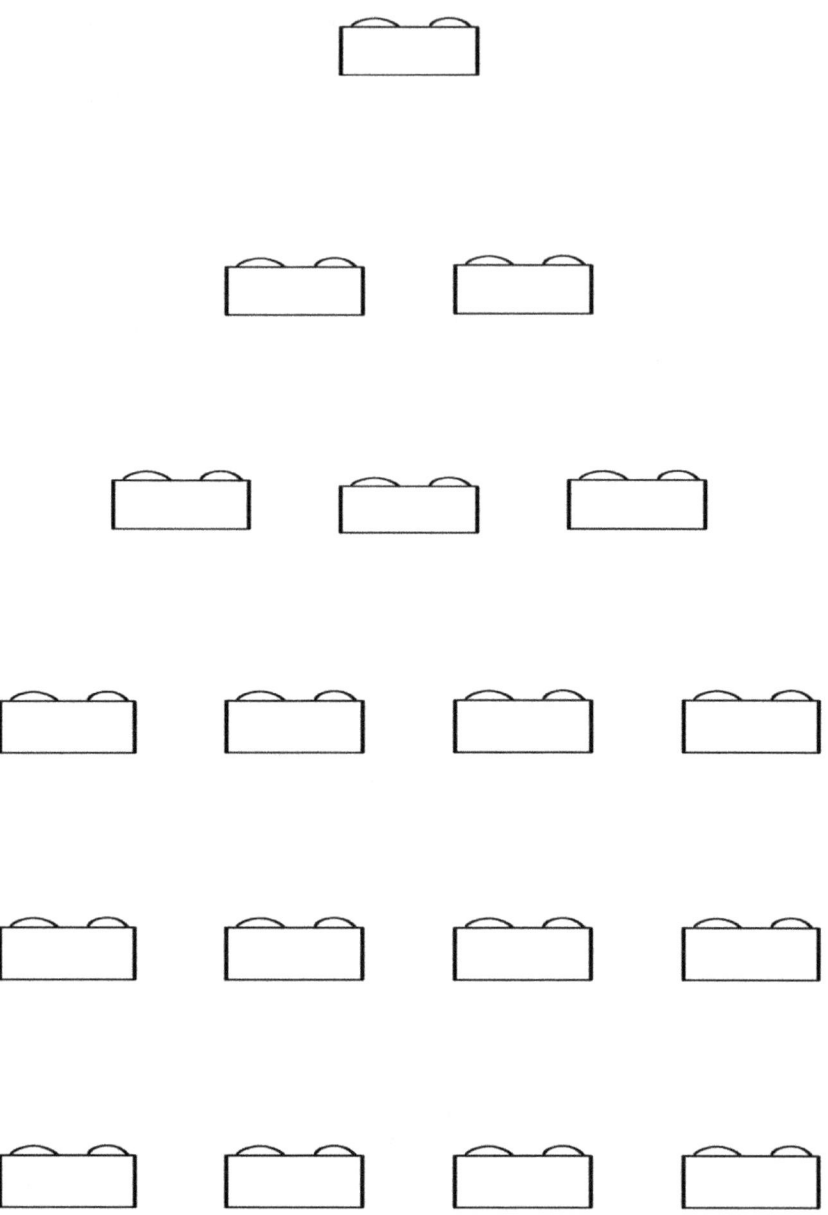

Figure 2.1 Building Blocks for Family Engagement

References

Alacam, N., & Olgan, R. (2017). Pre-service early childhood teachers' self-efficacy/beliefs towards parent involvement. *Teaching Education, 28,* 421–434. https://doi.org/10.1080/10476210.2017.1324843

Barnes, J. K., Guin, A., Allen, K., & Jolly, C. (2016). Engaging parents in early childhood education: Perspectives of childcare providers. *Family and Consumer Sciences Research Journal, 44,* 360–374. https://doi.org/10.1111/fcsr.12164

Bronfenbrenner, U. (1974). Developmental research, public policy, and the ecology of childhood. *Child Development, 45*(1), 1–5.

Brown, J. R., Knoche, L. L., Edwards, C. P., & Sheridan, S. M. (2009). Professional development to support parent engagement: A case study of early childhood practitioners. *Early Education & Development, 20,* 482–506. https://doi.org/10.1080/10409280902783475

Calzada, E. J., Huang, K., Hernandez, M., Soriano, E., Acra, C. F., Dawson-McClure, S., & Brotman, L. (2015). Family and teacher characteristics as predictors of parent involvement in education during early childhood among Afro-Caribbean and Latino immigrant families. *Urban Education, 50,* 870–896. https://doi.org/10.1177/0042085914534862

Demircan, Ö., & Erden, F. T. (2015). Parental involvement and developmentally appropriate practices: A comparison of parent and teacher beliefs. *Early Child Development and Care, 185,* 209–225. https://doi.org/10.1080/03004430.2014.919493

Epstein, J. L. (2001). *School, family, and community partnerships: Preparing educators and improving schools.* Boulder, CO: Westview Press.

Epstein, J. L., & Sheldon, S. B. (2016). Necessary but not sufficient: The role of policy for advancing programs of school, family, and community partnerships. *The Russell Sage Foundation Journal of the Social Sciences, 2*(5), 202–219. https://doi.org/10.7758/rsf.2016.2.5.10

Erdener, M. A., & Knoeppel, R. C. (2018). Parents' perceptions of their involvement in schooling. *International Journal of Research in Education and Science, 4,* 1–13. https://doi.org/10.21890/ijres.369197

Garbacz, S. A., McDowall, P. S., Schaughency, E., Sheridan, S. M., & Welch, G. W. (2015). A multidimensional examination of parent involvement across child and parent characteristics. *The Elementary School Journal, 115,* 384–406. https://doi.org/10.1086/680325

Ghiratto, L., & Mazzoni, V. (2013). Being part, being involved: The adult's role and child participation in an early childhood learning context. *International Journal of Early Years Education, 21*, 300–308. https://doi.org/10.1080/09669760.2013.867166

Goodall, J., & Montgomery, C. (2014). Parental involvement to parental engagement: A continuum. *Educational Review, 66*, 399–410. https://doi.org/10.1080.00131911.2013.781576

Halgunseth, L. C., Petereson, A., Stark, D. R., & Moodie, S. (2009). *Family engagement, diverse families, and early childhood education programs: An integrated review of the literature.* Retrieved from https://nieer.org/wp-content/uploads/2011/09/EDF_Literature20Review.pdf

Hilado, A. V., Kallemeyn, L., Leow, C., Lundy, M., & Israel, M. (2011). Supporting child welfare and parent involvement in preschool programs. *Early Childhood Education Journal, 39*, 343–353. https://doi.org/10.1007/s10643-011-0471-z

Hilado, A. V., Kallemeyn, L., & Phillips, L. (2013). Examining understandings of parent involvement in early childhood programs. *Early Childhood Research & Practice, 15*(2).

Hornby, G., & Lafaele, R. (2011). Barriers to parental involvement in education: An explanatory model. *Educational Review, 63*, 37–52. https://doi.org/10.1080/00131911.2018.1388612

Ihmeideh, F., & Oliemat, E. (2015). The effectiveness of family involvement in early childhood programmes: Perceptions of kindergarten principal and teachers. *Early Child Development and Care, 185*, 181–197. https://doi.org/10.1080/03004430.2014.915817

Knight-McKenna, M., & Hollingsworth, H. L. (2016). Fostering family – Teacher partnerships: Principles in practice. *Childhood Education, 92*, 383–390. https://doi.org/10.1080/00094056.2016.1226113

Ma, X., Shen, J., Krenn, H. Y., Hu, S., & Yuan, J. (2016). A meta-analysis of the relationship between learning outcomes and parental involvement during early childhood education and early elementary education. *Education Psychology Review, 28*, 771–801. https://doi.org/10.1007/s10648-015-9351-1

Mahmood, S. (2013). First-year preschool and kindergarten teachers: Challenges of working with parents. *School Community Journal, 23*(2), 55–85. Retrieved from https://files.eric.ed.gov/fulltext/EJ1028824.pdf

McNeal, R. B. (2015). Parent involvement and student performance: The influence of school context. *Educational Research for Policy and Practice, 14,* 153–167. https://doi.org/10.1007/s10671-014-9167-7

McWayne, C. M., & Melzi, G. (2014). Validation of a culture-contextualized measure of family engagement in the early learning of low-income Latino children. *Journal of Family Psychology, 28,* 260–266. https://doi.org/10.1037/a0036167

Mendez, J. L. (2010). How can parents get involved in preschool? Barriers and engagement in education by ethnic minority parents of children attending Head Start. *Cultural Diversity and Ethnic Minority Psychology, 16,* 26–36. https://doi.org/10.1037/a0016258

Morrison, J. W., Storey, P., & Zhang, C. (2015). Accessible family involvement in early childhood programs. *Dimensions of Early Childhood, 39*(3), 33–38. Retrieved from www.southernearlychildhood.org/upload/pdf/Accessible_Family_Involvement_in_Early_Childhood_Programs_by_Johnetta_W__Morrison_Pamela_Storey_and_Chenyi_Zhang.pdf

Murray, E., McFarland-Piazza, L., & Harrison, L. J. (2015). Changing patterns of parent-teacher communication and parent involvement from preschool to school. *Early Child Development and Care, 185,* 1031–1052. https://doi.org/10.1080/03004430.2014.975223

National Association for the Education of Young Children. (2010). *Engaging diverse families project.* Retrieved from www.naeyc.org/familyengagement/about

Nitecki, E. (2015). Integrated school-family partnerships in preschool: Building quality involvement through multidimensional relationships. *School Community Journal, 25,* 195–219. Retrieved from https://files.eric.ed.gov/fulltext/EJ1085725.pdf

No Child Left Behind Act of 2001, P.L. 107-110, 20 U.S.C. § 6319 (2002).

Sánchez, C., & Walsh, B. (2017). Meeting national expectations for partnering with families. *Dimensions of Early Childhood, 45*(2), 20–28. Retrieved from www.southernearlychildhood.org/page.php?purl=seca_publications

Schaub, M. (2015). Is there a home advantage in school readiness for young children? Trends in parent engagement in cognitive activities with young children, 1991–2001. *Journal of Early Childhood Research, 13,* 47–63. https://doi.org/10.1177/1476718X12468122

Share, M., & Kerrins, L. (2013). Supporting parental involvement in children's early learning: Lessons from community childcare centres in Dublin's Docklands. *Child Care in Practice, 19*, 355–374. https://doi.org/10.1080/13575279.2013.799457

Smetzer-Anderson, S., & Roessler, J. (2016). "Buy-in" vs. "allowed in": Lessons learned in family engagement program recruitment and retention. *Voices in Urban Education, 44*, 53–63. Retrieved from https://files.eric.ed.gov/fulltext/EJ1111064.pdf

Smith, S. C. (2014). Parental engagement in a Reggio Emilia-inspired Head Start program. *Early Childhood Research & Practice, 16*. Retrieved from http://ecrp.uiuc.edu/v16n1/smith.html

Summer, M., & Summer, G. L. (2014). Creating family learning communities. *YC: Young Children, 69*(4), 8–14. Retrieved from www.jstor.org/stable/ycyoungchildren.69.4.8

Tran, Y. (2014). Addressing reciprocity between families and schools: Why these bridges are instrumental for students' academic success. *Improving Schools, 17*, 18–29. https://doi.org /10.1177/1365480213515296

Weiss, H., Caspe, M., & Lopez, M. E. (2006). *Family involvement in early childhood education*. Cambridge, MA: Harvard University, Harvard Family Research Project.

Whyte, K. L., & Karabon, A. (2016). Transforming teacher – Family relationships: Shifting roles and perceptions of home visits through the Funds of Knowledge approach. *Early Years: Journal of International Research & Development, 36*(2), 207. https://doi.org/10.1080/09575146.2016.1139546

Winder, C., & Corter, C. (2016). The influence of prior experiences on early childhood education students' anticipated work with families. *Teaching and Teacher Education, 55*, 133–142. https://doi.org/10.1016/j.tate.2016.01.005

Zhang, Q. (2015). Defining "meaningfulness": Enabling preschoolers to get the most out of parental involvement. *Australasian Journal of Early Childhood, 40*(4), 112–120. Retrieved from www.researchgate.net/profile/Qilong_Zhang3/publication/291835715_Defining_'meaningfulness'_Enabling_preschoolers_to_get_the_most_out_of_parental_involvement/links/56b09e3608ae9f0ff7b60ff7/Defining-meaningfulness-Enabling-preschoolers-to-get-the-most-out-of-parental-involvement.pdf

Building a Comprehensive System for Family Engagement

The final principle outlined by NAEYC (2010) indicates that practitioners create, implement, and support a comprehensive family engagement system. What is meant by a *comprehensive system*? A system is a set of things (people, events, activities, and such) that are *interconnected* in ways that produce their own patterns of behavior over time (Goffin & Washington, 2019). In this context, family engagement is a system in which practitioners, families, and others define and refine the patterns of behavior and expectations. The development of *policies and procedures* provides the foundation for these patterns.

Why are we starting with the final principle? As stated earlier, family policies should be as integral to the ECE program's operation as those regarding tuition, regulations, and other procedures. All the components discussed in Chapter 2 work together to create this comprehensive system. Epstein and Sanders (2006) defined comprehensive systems as the spheres of influence that overlap between educational programs, families, and the community. They might look like the example in Figure 3.1. Such a system's central foundation should focus on the interpersonal relationships and information exchange among all members (Epstein & Sanders, 2006).

As outlined in Chapter 2, children learn in the home, the educational program, and the community, thus creating the need for the families, practitioners, and community members to collaborate to support learning and development (Epstein & Sheldon, 2016). It is not enough to mandate engagement as a requirement – as loosely indicated in an "open door policy." There must be research-based practices in place among the members

Building a Comprehensive System

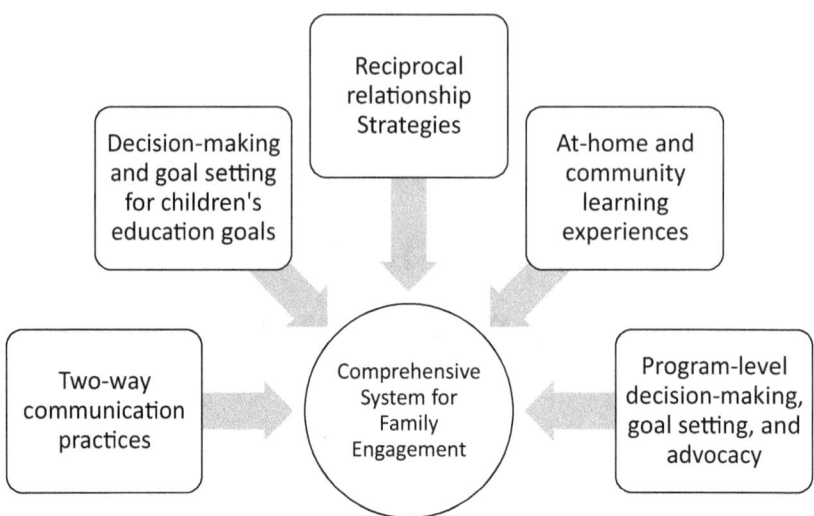

Figure 3.1 Components of a Comprehensive System of Family Engagement

to implement and plan a meaningful delivery system (Epstein & Sheldon, 2016; Fantuzzo et al., 2013).

It is essential to build the system based on the family's diverse factors such as age, family culture background, philosophy, experience, and opportunities available within the program and community (Epstein & Sanders, 2006; Morrison, Storey, & Zhang, 2015). Policies and procedures should be fluid and not a "one size fits all" approach. The policy should contain a continuous review component, making adjustments when the members' characteristics and composition change (Goodall & Montgomery, 2014; Morrison et al., 2015; Murray, McFarland-Piazza, & Harrison, 2015). The policies and procedures must reflect that not all families are the same, not all have the same needs, and all face different challenges regarding their participation in their child's education (Goodall & Montgomery, 2014; Murray et al., 2015).

Using the NAEYC Principles of Family Engagement as a guideline, practitioners can develop policies and procedures to address families and the field's changing needs. Policies and procedures should enhance child growth and development and the home–program–community relationship (Fantuzzo et al., 2013; Nitecki, 2015; Stefanski, Valli, & Jacobson, 2016). When high-quality family engagement practices are implemented and supported, families become empowered consumers rather than clients who only receive services (Jor'dan, Wolf, & Douglass, 2012; Sherwood & Nind, 2014; Stefanski et al., 2016).

Why Policy?

According to Merriam Webster, policies provide a "definite course or method of action" used "to guide and determine present and future decisions." To implement the course of action, a "high-level overall plan," which provides an understanding of certain assurances, is created (www.merriam-webster.com/dictionary/policy). Policies are an implied contract between the program's practitioners and the family, which outlines what each member is tasked with by defining roles and responsibilities. In short, policies are *action plans*. As you work through each section of the policy development, you will address the reasons the policy exists, as well as the roles each member will play. As mentioned in Chapter 1, you will be developing two different policies. For families, you will describe each of the principles from their perspective – what it means for them and what they will need to do as members of your program. These policies will also address what practitioners will need to do to support the child and the family. In other words, you are clearly defining each step in each principle to ensure everyone is on the same page and understands what is expected of them.

Policy development should include carefully addressing the following components as needed:

- A description of how the curriculum reflects family values, beliefs, and experiences. For example, when providing activities for learning at home, are all children represented in each activity? Are you sending home activities that represent and value all families? All activities should represent the culture and climate of the families you serve.
- A explanation and connection to how the program incorporates families' home languages into all aspects of the program – do you provide communications such as your monthly newsletter in their language? Do you have access to interpreters or other materials to assist them with this? Are your classrooms reflective of several languages to represent not only your family's but the languages of others in your community?

- A description of the collaborative nature of the family–practitioner partnership – what does collaboration mean? The definition is basically *working together* with a person or persons toward a common goal. The common goal, as defined by the purpose of family engagement, is the child's educational success. Later in this book, you will delve into the component of collaborative, reciprocal relationships.
- A description of how the program will communicate with the family about the child's academic progress and in general. Communication, as you will see further into the book, has many moving parts. As pointed out in Chapter 2, families need to be invited to participate. Often, they want to but do not know how! Having a policy will give them a good idea of what is expected. Still, it is reliant upon the practitioners to extend the invitation.
- A description of how families can help – from planning an event or activity to volunteer opportunities or supporting learning activities in the classroom. The intent is to find out how to meet families' needs and capabilities to engage. In Appendix B, you will find a sample survey to include with the Intake Survey to determine each family's preferences for engagement.
- A description of specific communication practices and forms and how practitioners will distribute them. The forms in Appendix A will assist you with gaining information on how families want to communicate and be communicated with, along with a way to track communications.

Additionally, you will address the fundamental questions of *"who, what, where, when, why, and how"* introduced in Chapter 1. A brief overview of how you will want to address each of these follows.

Who Is the Policy For?

The first step in engaging the family is to help them understand their role in their child's education and as members of the program's community. The program's Vision and Mission statement should clearly define this role. If your program does not have a Vision and Mission statement, you will create or revise them in Chapter 4. Perhaps the most critical aspect of making program policy is to reflect on the families currently enrolled in your program – who are your clients?

The families you serve are likely from the Millennial generation. It is essential to know this, as family values and beliefs change over time as society changes. Bronfenbrenner's (1974) ecological systems theory (Figure 3.2) reflects how these changes affect the child and the family.

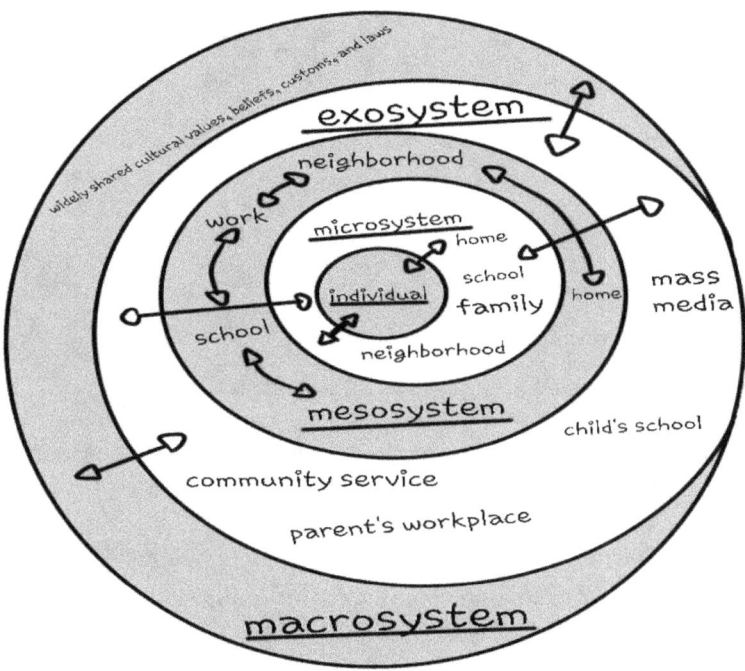

Figure 3.2 Bronfenbrenner's Ecological Systems Theory (1974)

Kathryn E. McKay

Families' beliefs about engaging with the child's educational program over the last three decades are compared in the following chart (Gross & O'Neil, 2017, as cited in Koralek et al. (2019)).

The chart measures the level of involvement needed as perceived by parents in each generation. While a 10% difference may not seem significant, it indicates that interest is rising. Now, *more than half* of millennial families believe that they can never be "too involved" in their child's *education* as opposed to those from the Gen X and Baby Boomer generations. This leads to the question, *"If we know they want to be involved, why aren't we helping them do so?"*

For the millennial generation and those that follow, we must also recognize how the family dynamic has changed. Today's families are no longer

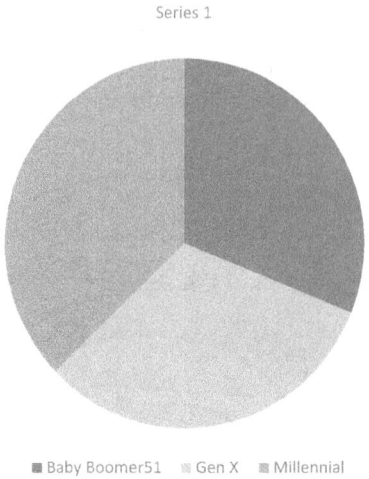

Figure 3.3 Family Interest in Engagement 3 Generations

the nuclear, traditional, married mom and dad with two children model but have expanded to include the following:

- Adoptive families, consisting of one or more nonbiological children.
- Nontraditional families, such as an older sibling as legal guardian or grandparents as guardians.
- Extended families, consisting of one parent and at least one child related to them and also living with someone else who may be related/ unrelated to them (grandparent, aunt, uncle, cousin, sibling, etc.).
- Multi-generational families, consisting of three or more generations living in one home.
- Foster families, consisting of one or more nonbiological children in the home with or without biological children of their own.
- Divorced families with children moving between two separate households on a regular basis.
- Blended families, consisting of parents who have remarried, brining biological or adoptive children from the prior relationship to live together in one home.
- Unmarried families, consisting of two individuals who are not married, not related, but live together; children may be biologically related to one or both individuals or adopted.

Building a Comprehensive System

- Single-parent families (either mom or dad), consisting of only one parent living in the home; may be biological, foster, step, grandparent, or adoptive.
- Same-sex families consisting of parents who are married or unmarried of the same biological sex; children may be biological, step, or adopted.
- Subfamilies are families who live in the home of another family because of extraneous circumstances.

This list is not exhaustive for including all the different types of families you will be serving. To further understand the families you serve, you must factor in the stressors included in Bronfenbrenner's systems theory. According to Carter and McGoldrick (2005), there are vertical stressors and horizontal stressors within each system in each family's life cycle. See the following chart to see the stressors as they relate to the Bronfenbrenner ecological systems theory.

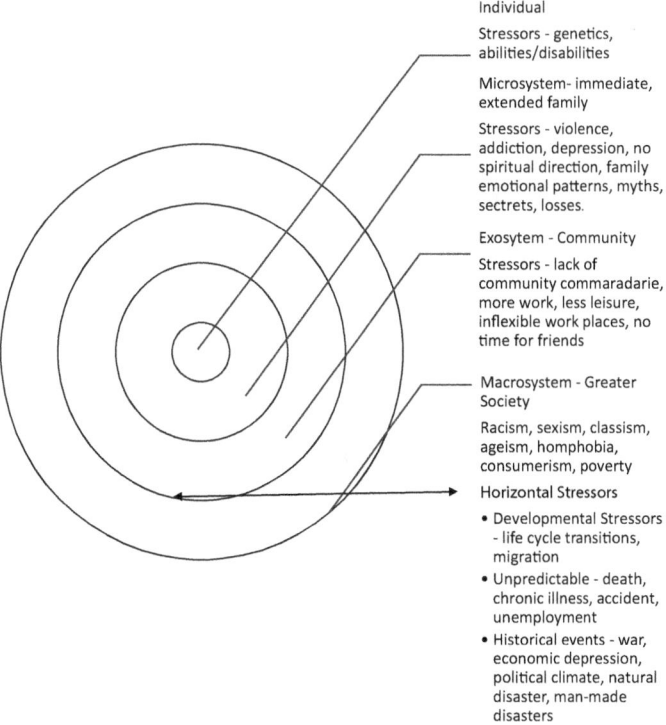

Figure 3.4 Family Stressors

In addition to the stressors outlined by Carter and McGoldrick, we must also consider poverty, homelessness, military deployments, and migrant and immigration status. The possible combinations of challenges and stresses that can affect families are vast. It is critical, then, to know and understand your families to build appropriate engagement policies to meet *their* needs. Respecting their situations and needs is the very core of family-engagement partnerships. How might these dynamics of differing family structures affect the creation of your policy? Throughout the development of each policy, you will likely include the information you have learned about each family from the intake surveys. Ask yourself, "How much do I really know about my families?" Have you asked for this information? When we **do not ask,** we are, in fact, disrespecting their culture and family values, beliefs, traditions, and situations.

In the same way, it is imperative to look at the practitioners in your program. What characteristics do they bring to your program's dynamic? In what ways are they similar, and in what ways are they different? In developing the practitioners' policy, consider their values, beliefs, and cultural background to identify potential areas that might conflict with your overall engagement practices. Each practitioner will need to examine themselves in the light of the Bronfenbrenner, Carter, and McGoldrick "lens" to first understand and identify what they are bringing to the table. To fully incorporate the practitioner's contributions and needs, it will be useful to work together through this portion of policy together. Think about their part in each area – how do they contribute to and support the program's mission and vision statement? What are their responsibilities in building meaningful relationships? How are they tasked with communicating with families and administration? How will they be expected to connect learning at home and in the community? How will they assist families in the decision-making and goal-setting process? How can they support families in program engagement and advocacy? Perhaps the most critical question is how the practitioner team will work together to support this policy for family engagement, help with the implementation process, and adhere to their role.

While the "who" section may seem simple at the start, it is imperative to connect the *"who"* to your policy's foundation. You cannot identify the other components of *"what, where, when, how, or why"* until you know **who**. It will be necessary to identify this aspect first as you develop each section of your policy. Start brainstorming now as you read through the rest of these questions. Remember, these are just the basics to get you going. You can use the illustration on the next page to document the characteristics of the families you serve based on the information shared thus far. Start brainstorming as to how these might fit into each piece of your engagement policy.

Building a Comprehensive System

Figure 3.5 All Kinds of Families

Kathryn E. McKay

What Is Needed to Implement Policy?

Planning is an essential component for implementing any policy or procedure. As you begin the development process by identifying the "who," you will want to start a planning chart and timeline for implementation. The worksheets in each chapter are for your note-gathering and brainstorming practice. Again, family members and practitioners must work together with the administration to develop these. When you invite their participation, you support communication, relationship building, and program-level decision making. Together you can identify the need for each principle's policy. The planning process will include breaking down each policy component and identifying the critical tasks, roles, responsibilities, and timeline for completion.

The "what" for each policy is likely going to look different – each policy is connected to a goal. Ask yourself and others – *what* is the goal (purpose)? What will it look like when it is fully implemented and operational? You will start with your vision and mission statements – what does your program need to do to visually support these goals? When a family reads each statement, do they see them in action? To build relationships with families, *what* strategies will you use? *What* do these relationships look like? In the policy about communication, you will need to identify *what* communications you will use, *what* information will be shared, and *what* formats. In return, *what* types of communication do you want from families and in *what* forms? *What* activities will be provided for learning at home, and *what* community learning activities can be shared or sponsored by your program? To get families fully engaged in educational decision making and goal setting for their child, *what* do they need to know? *What* information will you need to share with them? *What* format will this take? *What* kind of engagement do you want from families at the program level? *What* kind of advocacy do you want families and practitioners to engage in? Once you have identified all of the *"what's"*, you can then go back and start making the *"who"* connections for each.

Where Will the Implementation Occur?

An often-overlooked component of implementing policy is deciding where each policy component "belongs." In general, *where* is this policy going to

Building a Comprehensive System

be located? Is it separate from your parent or practitioner handbooks or predominately displayed first in them? *Where* can both new and existing families find them? *Where* are the Vision and Mission statements located? *Where* will relationship-building occur? *Where* can families expect to find communications in all formats? For example, you may create a family information and resource center to access communications, educational materials, and resources. *Where* can practitioners sit and have a private conversation with a family aside from drop-off and pick-up times in the classroom?

The *"where"* or location of learning at home and in the community may seem obvious. However, families and practitioners need to know *where* the activities or information are located for ease of access. *Where* will families and practitioners meet for decision making and goal setting? For example, you have decided that part of your policy for including the family is conducting parent conferences. *Where* will these take place? In the classroom, the conference room, or another area? For each principle, you will determine "where" each one will take place. *Where* can families become engaged in the program-level decision making and goal setting? *Where* are the opportunities to serve as advocates? As you work through each principle and policy, it is crucial to define "where" for both families and practitioners. As with addressing the *"what"* with the *"who,"* – *who* will determine the *where* and *what* is needed for each? As you are beginning to see, there is an overlap and a pattern forming. For each step forward, you will need to re-examine the prior ones to make the necessary adjustments for sound policies and procedures.

When Will Each Component Be Implemented?

Now you can fine-tune the planning process for each principle, providing a more concrete *"when"* each one will occur. *When* will the policy be implemented? *When* and how often will it be reviewed? *When* will families and practitioners have opportunities to build relationships? *When* can families expect communication from the practitioners and vice versa? For example, you have created a policy to distribute a newsletter to the families. *When* will this be delivered to them – weekly, monthly, or in another time frame? *When* are practitioners expected to complete the newsletter? *When* and how often can families expect learning activities to be sent home? *When* are the community opportunities available to them? *When* can they meet with practitioners to make decisions and set goals? *When* will practitioners be expected to meet with families? In the previous example of parent conferences, *when* will they be held? *When* will families have opportunities to engage in program-level decisions and goals? *When* can they engage in advocacy? Each section of the policy must identify the *"when"* and consider families' time and availability. Understanding *when* something will happen supports accountability in the family/practitioner partnership as well.

How Will Each Component Be Implemented?

It is critical to define the "how" for each policy – thoroughly describing each member of the partnership's actions and roles. Families and practitioners must have detailed information to know and understand their role and what they must do to support the policy. Each policy must clearly define the expectations of each member of the partnership. *How* are partnerships going to be formed? In each policy, you will likely think back and address the *"what"* a bit further – *what* are the responsibilities for each role? *How* will communications be delivered – again, meeting families where they are. From the newsletter example, the policy should state how the newsletter will be provided – in paper format, through email, posted on the program's website, or a combination. *How* will learning activities be provided for in-home use? *How* will families know what to do with them? You will likely think back to *what* they will need to use them.

How will families be linked to learning opportunities in the community? *How* will they be involved in the decision-making and goal-setting process for their child's education? Using the parent conference example, *how* are practitioners expected to conduct them, and *how* is the family expected to participate? *How* can families participate in the program's decision-making and goal-setting process? *How* can they advocate for their child and the field? *How* can they be involved in the process of making these policies? The *"how"* likely will be the largest component of each policy. This is where each piece will start to come together. At this point, there might be some redundancy, and that is a **good** thing. The more brainstorming and idea writing you do, the better you can fine-tune the policy. It is better to have more to work with to shape the policy into what it needs to be.

Explaining the "Why" of Each Policy

While it may seem that the *"why"* should be the first question, and it is, it is more important to understand how it works throughout the policy-building process. Each of the prior components will connect the *"why." Why* do we need a family engagement policy? *Why* is there a need for a clear Vision and Mission statement? *Why* must we develop this "comprehensive system?" *Why* do we need to support relationships and build partnerships? *Why* must we improve and fine-tune our communication practices? *Why* do we need to provide learning activities and connect families to learning experiences in the community? *Why* should families be involved in the decision-making and goal-setting process for their child? *Why* should we engage families to assist at the program level and in advocacy efforts?

To answer all of these *"why's"* – if you are unsure of any of them – refer back to Chapter 2. The research tells us why this is important – to support families and children in the educational journey. To work together as a team. In lesson planning, practitioners describe the "why" for each activity goal, explaining why it is appropriate and relevant for learning. Ideally, these are connected to researched information such as the developmental domains milestones or state early learning standards.

In the same way, each policy should clearly define its value. It is human nature, regardless of age or developmental status, to want to know *"why."* Our job is to connect each member of the partnership to understand *"what"* is in it for them and *why* it must be done. When every member understands the *"why"* and has **ownership in it**, it is more likely the entire process will be successful from introduction to implementation to follow-through.

To review, as you go through each of the following components of family engagement policy, you will address:

- *Who* – is involved, affected, responsible?
- *What* – materials, equipment, formats are needed?
- *Where* – will it be located, completed, achieved?
- *When* – will it happen, occur, be expected?
- *How* – will each member be expected to perform? How will the policy be implemented, benefit each member of the partnership, and support the family/child/practitioner?
- *Why* – is it needed, are we doing this, policy?

As you are forming your policies throughout this process, keep in mind the following general "truths" about families in general and the families you serve.

- All families have hopes, dreams, and goals for their child/children. They will differ in their beliefs, values, and efforts in how to support those goals.
- It is imperative to know and understand how to support families in their homes. While you may not physically visit the house, you can still provide supplemental activities to connect learning between home and the program.
- As outlined in Bronfenbrenner's ecological systems theory (1974), it is also imperative to connect to the community for both families and practitioners. By participating in these events and connecting families to events that can further support them in raising their children, the partnership circle has been expanded.
- Embrace the fact that families are the child's first and primary teacher. This does not mean that there will not be areas in which conflicts will arise. It means that the relationship is open, and the members of the partnership can feel free to share ideas and find ways to compromise when conflicts occur. Respecting the family members in this way empowers them to do and learn more.
- Remember, family engagement's *primary* purpose is to support the child's education in all developmental areas.
- Even with the best supportive policies, family engagement is a process, not just a program of activities. It will require ongoing energy and effort.
- Families' interaction with their own children is an integral component of the engagement process. Every practitioner within the program must recognize the value, diversity, and difficulties each family faces within their role.
- Most of the barriers that prevent engagement primarily originate on the program side, not the family side. An example is *time* – families only have so much time they can afford to use. It is up to the program to accommodate the engagement relationship based on individual families' time needs.
- There will be moments when family members or practitioners may seem "hard to reach." Everyone needs to meet each other "where they

are" – with no bias regarding gender, ethnicity, family circumstance, education, or income.
- Successful engagement involves nurturing relationships and partnerships.

In the following chapters, you will write about these questions for each policy. You will find an example and a blank worksheet to create your policy outline in the following chapters. Remember to make each one as a **team** with family members and practitioners who work with the children and families daily (outside of administration). Although examples are provided, it is imperative to make each section **fit your families, practitioners, and program's needs.** Appendices D, E, and F have an **outline** for both family and practitioner policy and an example outline for your complete policy final draft.

To get your creative juices flowing, I want to share that whenever I see the *"who, what, where, when, how, and why"* questions, I think of the old Abbott and Costello routine *Who's on First?* As you work through, some questions will be easy to answer, and others will not. In keeping with the baseball theme introduced in Chapter 1, further define your *"Field of Dreams"* using the illustration on the next page to start answering some of these questions. It will be essential to address the ones outside of the basics mentioned earlier, too, as you work through each policy building block. There will be many times the team will ask, "Why do we give a darn?" or feel like "I don't know" the answers – and it is okay. That is where your policy will grow.

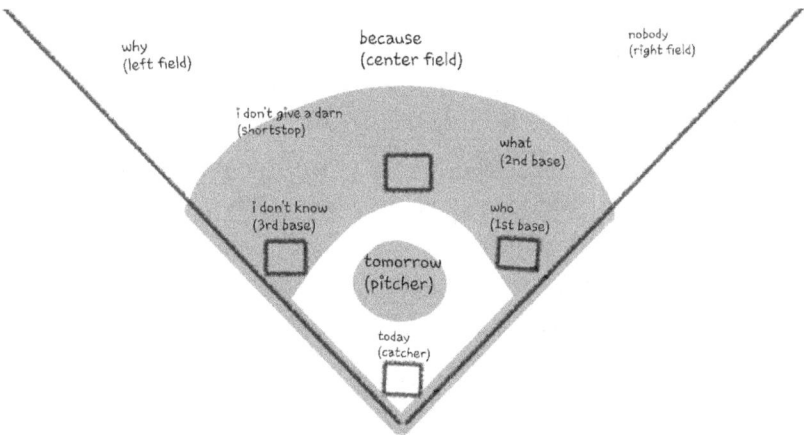

Figure 3.6 Who's on First

Kathryn E. McKay

References

Bronfenbrenner, U. (1974). Developmental research, public policy, and the ecology of childhood. *Child development, 45*(1), 1–5.

Carter, B., & McGoldrick, M. (2005). *Overview: The expanded family life cycle: Individual, family, and social perspectives.* Retrieved from https://sw2.haifa.ac.il/images/stories/Field_studies/family_1.pdf

Epstein, J. L., & Sanders, M. G. (2006). Prospects for change: Preparing educators for school, family, and community partnerships. *Peabody Journal of Education, 81*(2), 81–120. https://doi.org/10.1207/S15327930pje8108_5

Epstein, J. L., & Sheldon, S. B. (2016). Necessary but not sufficient: The role of policy for advancing programs of school, family, and community partnerships. *The Russell Sage Foundation Journal of the Social Sciences, 2*(5), 202–219. https://doi.org/10.7758/rsf.2016.2.5.10

Fantuzzo, J., Gadsden, V., Li, F., Sproul, F., McDermott, P., Hightower, D., & Minney, A. (2013). Multiple dimensions of family engagement in early childhood education: Evidence for a short form of the Family Involvement Questionnaire. *Early Childhood Research Quarterly, 28*, 734–742. https://doi.org/10.1016/j.ecresq.2013.07.001

Goffin, S. G., & Washington, V. (2019). *Ready or not: Early care and education's leadership choices 12 years later.* New York, NY: Teacher's College Press.

Goodall, J., & Montgomery, C. (2014). Parental involvement to parental engagement: A continuum. *Educational Review, 66*, 399–410. https://doi.org/10.1080.00131911.2013.781576

Jor'dan, J. R., Wolf, K. G., & Douglass, A. (2012). Increasing family engagement in early childhood programs. *Young Children, 67*(5), 18–23. Retrieved from www.naeyc.org

Koralek, D., Nemeth, K., & Ramsey, K. (2019). *Families and educators together: Building great relationships that support young children.* Washington, DC: NAEYC.

Morrison, J. W., Storey, P., & Zhang, C. (2015). Accessible family involvement in early childhood programs. *Dimensions of Early Childhood, 39*(3), 33–38. Retrieved from www.southernearlychildhood.org/upload/

pdf/Accessible_Family_Involvement_in_Early_Childhood_Programs_by_Johnetta_W_Morrison_Pamela_Storey_and_Chenyi_Zhang.pdf

Murray, E., McFarland-Piazza, L., & Harrison, L. J. (2015). Changing patterns of parent-teacher communication and parent involvement from preschool to school. *Early Child Development and Care, 185*, 1031–1052. https://doi.org/10.1080/03004430.2014.975223

National Association for the Education of Young Children. (2010). *Engaging diverse families project.* Retrieved from www.naeyc.org/familyengagement/about

Nitecki, E. (2015). Integrated school-family partnerships in preschool: Building quality involvement through multidimensional relationships. *School Community Journal, 25*, 195–219. Retrieved from https://files.eric.ed.gov/fulltext/EJ1085725.pdf

Sherwood, G., & Nind, M. A. (2014). Parents' experiences of support: Co-constructing their stories. *International Journal of Early Years Education, 22*, 457–470. https://doi.org/10.1080/09669760.2014.970520

Stefanski, A., Valli, L., & Jacobson, R. (2016). Beyond involvement and engagement: The role of the family in school – Community partnerships. *School Community Journal, 26*, 135–160. Retrieved from https://files.eric.ed.gov/fulltext/EJ1124001.pdf

4 Beginning With the End in Mind

Vision and Mission Statements

In the previous chapters, you have learned about the components that support – or will be the foundation of – a comprehensive family engagement system. Goffin and Washington (2007) posed this question: what is the ECE field's defining intent? Carter and Curtis (2010, pp. 39–40) addressed some possibilities:

- Providing a service for working families.
- Providing children a head start for later academic success.
- Enhancing young children's self-concept and the social skills needed to interact in the world.
- Creating a community for adults and children to experience connection.
- Ensuring childhood is complete with play, adventure, and exploration.

Further, Bruno (2008) provided concepts to apply to creating a Vision and Mission for your ECE program. I have adapted and described them to guide your work on the Vision and Mission statements.

- Everyone who reads or hears it should be *inspired* by it.
- Practitioners should be empowered to find their *own purpose* in the field.
- When negative issues arise, the Vision and Mission should stand firm and guide everyone back "to shore" like a lighthouse.
- Sets the program's standards for quality implementation and practice.

DOI: 10.4324/9781003133353-4

- Represents the core values *of best practices*.
- Every decision made within the program should be grounded in these two statements.
- They should not be time bound. You may change things here and there as practices and theory dictate but, by and large, they should be able to be timeless.

It is now time for you to build the next layer of the *foundation* of engagement policy. Every business should know the end goal – what is it that the company exists for, as discussed earlier. This is what the Vision and Mission statements are all about. Looking at the end goals and figuring out how to get there – a road map, so to speak. What is your purpose for existence? What do you want families to know about your people and program? Keep in mind that *policy* is an action plan. Part of that plan is defining the program's priorities, the resources needed to support those priorities, and ensuring that every team member works toward the team's shared goals. The Vision and Mission statements provide a platform for developing the goals and objectives of the overall program. Think of these two statements as a road map to the road map of your program's goals and objectives, including policy. In other words, you cannot create an individual policy without understanding where that policy fits into your program. Thus, because we are developing a policy for family engagement, the focus for your Vision and Mission statements is the child and the family.

The Vision and Mission statements will give the family a preview of what they can expect from your program and practitioners. Based on your exercise results in Chapter 3, who are your families, and what is your *vision* for them? The definition of the word "vision" includes "a thought, concept, or object formed by the imagination" (www.merriam-webster.com/dictionary/vision). Thus, your vision statement should produce a clear mental picture of the concepts of the program. This statement will likely be one of the first things the family will read. If you do not currently have a vision statement, this would be a great time to create one!

A vision statement should represent your program's purpose and core values – your overall long-term goal that guides and directs all other actions of the program. What are the values you *treasure most* for families and children? It could be viewed as your tagline, or, more importantly, it reveals your program's *destination* (remember, road map!). It defines the end *goal*

Beginning With the End in Mind

Figure 4.1 Crystal Ball of Vision

Kathryn E. McKay

of the children's and families' participation in your program. When they leave your program, what will they have accomplished? Think about your vision for your program – the mental image you want families to have when they read it. Use the crystal ball in Figure 4.1 and write down your thoughts using descriptive words, and think about the *"who, what, when, where, how, and why"* questions from Chapter 3. These thoughts and ideas will help you develop a cohesive vision statement, which will be further defined in the mission statement.

The following is the vision statement I created for my program.

Hands On Learning Preschool: where children, families, and educators grow and learn together through play every day!

This statement demonstrates that families are engaged with their children and the practitioners in the growth and learning process. It covers each of the family engagement principles – through four critical words – **grow and learn together**. When families read that statement, I have subconsciously planted the seed for relationship building. They also have a clear idea of our purpose and how we plan to achieve that purpose – grow and learn together **through play**.

To create your vision statement – you must first define your program's purpose (end goal), who is involved or included, and how it will be achieved. I have provided an example of the process below.

Creating a Vision Statement

Family Handbook Vision Statement Include all the details needed for families to know what your vision is for them and their child.	**Practitioner Handbook Vision Statement** Include all the details needed for program employees to know how to support the vision.
WHY: to provide families the overall goal of enrolling in our program.	**WHY:** to help all practitioners support the overall goal for the families and children.
WHO: all children, families?	**WHO:** practitioners
WHAT: a concise statement that explains what we want the children and families to achieve throughout their time in the program.	**WHAT:** a detailed explanation of what the vision means.
WHERE: located on all marketing material, described in the family handbook. The vision should be evidenced in all practices.	**WHERE:** in practitioner handbook, posted in common practitioner areas. The vision should be evidenced in all practices.
WHEN: ongoing. The vision should be evidenced in all other aspects of the program. It should be prominently used as your primary marketing tool.	**WHEN:** ongoing. The vision should be evidenced in all practices.
HOW: once formulated, all other policies and procedures should support the vision. Monitor through family surveys.	**HOW:** the vision should be the driving force behind all practitioner actions. Monitor and reevaluate current practices regularly to ensure the vision is supported.
VISION STATEMENT: A place (our program, where) **children, families, and practitioners (who), grow and learn (what) through play (how) every day (when).**	

The Mission Statement

Once the vision statement has been created, the mission statement will further define the vision's objectives. The vision statement describes *why* we exist – why we do the things outlined in our program handbook. The mission statement, then, explains *how* we do it. The mission should contain action verbs and descriptions of how the vision will be accomplished. Think about the vision you have just created and about how it will relate to working with families in your program. Where and how will they become engaged? Remember the guidance from the principles about engaging families (NAEYC, 2010):

- Families need to help with decision making and goal setting – *how* will you include them?
- We need reciprocal relationships with families – *how* will you meet all families where they are and develop these relationships?
- You will need two-way communication – *how* will you provide communication, and *how* do you expect families to communicate back to you?
- Families need connections for learning at home and in the community – *how* will these activities be provided, implemented, or connected?
- Families need help with decision making, goal setting, and engaging in advocacy at the program level – specifically, *how* can families get involved in your program and advocacy activities?

Once these questions have been answered, you can formulate the ideas into a cohesive statement. The mission statement describes the program's *purpose* and *core values*. It is a **current view** of what can be expected by the families in one to two short, concise paragraphs. In the previous example, the vision is to grow and learn together – how is this accomplished? What are the specific actions to accomplish each aspect? As you think about creating policies for family engagement, think about how you have already included (or need) the following information:

- What is your program's philosophy of how children learn, and how is it demonstrated?
- What can families expect to see children doing?
- What can families expect to DO as part of this?

In other words, what do you do, how do you do it, and who does it benefit? – who are you doing it for?

I have provided my mission statement in the following paragraphs. Paragraph one outlines our educational philosophy (our purpose and core values). Paragraph two gives a brief description of what we do and *how it will be provided*.

> Hands On Learning Preschool exists to provide children and their families with stimulating and developmentally appropriate experiences. These experiences support the physical, intellectual, linguistic, and emotional/social domains of growth and learning. Our teachers provide these experiences daily in a natural environment, helping children's natural desire and curiosity to explore the world around them. We consider the child's family, both immediate and extended, vital to the learning process. We strive to meet all families where they are in their ability to engage through various activities, events, and play-based experiences with their child.
>
> In these daily experiences, children spend most of their day exploring specific interest areas – Creative Art, Math, Blocks, Language/Literacy, Science/Discovery, and Dramatic Play. Through these experiences, they learn the foundational skills needed for higher learning and critical thinking. We engage families in this process by providing information on developmental milestones, the state Early Learning Guidelines, and supplemental activities completed at home in various ways. We will also connect families to learning experiences outside of our program. We ask families to provide us with information on their values, beliefs, and desires for their child's learning. In turn, we will provide various forms and means of communication to inform families of their child's growth and development. Families are encouraged to partner with their child's teachers, administrators, community members, and policymakers to fully support the growth and development process.

Here is the breakdown of how each component is addressed based on our definition of the mission statement:

- **Purpose and Core Value:** hands On Learning Preschool exists to *provide children and their families experiences that are stimulating and developmentally appropriate*.
- **Core Value:** these experiences *support the physical, intellectual, linguistic, and emotional/social domains of growth and learning.*

- **Core Value:** our teachers provide these experiences daily in a natural environment, supporting *children's natural desire and curiosity to explore the world around them.*
- **Core Value:** we consider the child's *family, both immediate and extended, vital to the learning process.*
- **Core Value:** we strive to meet all families where they are in their ability to engage through various activities, events, and play-based experiences with their child.

The purpose and core values clearly define how we will begin the relationship process with families and describe our educational philosophy for them – the first connections to help them better understand decision making and goal setting. We have provided a road map to *engagement*. The second half of the statement describes *how* the vision, purpose, and core values will be implemented using action statements.

- **How can families help with decision making and goal setting?** *We ask families to provide us with information on their values, beliefs, and desires for their child's learning. Families are encouraged to partner with their child's teachers, administrators, community members, and policymakers to fully support the growth and development process.*
- **How do we meet families where they are and form reciprocal relationships?** *Families are encouraged to partner with their child's teachers, administrators, community members, and policymakers to fully support the growth and development process.*
- **How will you provide communication, and how do you expect families to communicate back to you?** *We ask families to provide us with information on their values, beliefs, and desires for their child's learning. In turn, we will provide various forms and means of communication to inform families of their child's growth and development. Families are encouraged to partner with their child's teachers, administrators, community members, and policymakers to fully support the growth and development process.*
- **How will families be connected to learning at home and in the community?** *We engage families in this process by providing information on developmental milestones, the state early learning guidelines, and supplemental activities completed at home in various ways. We will also connect families to learning experiences outside of our program.*

- **How will we encourage families to engage in decision making, goal setting, and advocacy at the program?** *Families are encouraged to partner with their child's teachers, administrators, community members, and policymakers to fully support the growth and development process.*

Using the same format as the vision statement, work through the process to determine where your mission statement needs work, where it can be revised or completely revamped. Sometimes, we need to start fresh. An example of what this process might look like is provided on the following page.

Creating a Mission Statement

Parent Handbook Mission Statement Include all the details needed for families to know what your mission is for them and their child.	Practitioner Handbook Vision Statement Include all the details needed for program employees to know how to support the mission.
WHY: to clarify the details of the vision and let families know what the program is about, along with the educational philosophy.	**WHY:** to clarify the philosophy of the program and foundation for practice.
WHO: ideally, the mission is intended for all families, practitioners, and community members.	**WHO:** the mission is for families, practitioners, and community members.
WHAT: defines the purpose of the program and its educational philosophy from the family perspective.	**WHAT:** defines the purpose of the program and the educational philosophy from the practitioner perspective.
WHERE: in the family handbook, posted clearly in common areas.	**WHERE:** in the practitioner handbook, policies, and procedures, posted clearly in common areas.
WHEN: ongoing. The mission is applied to all practices.	**WHEN:** ongoing. The mission is applied to all practices.
HOW: ongoing, evidenced through practice. Monitor through family surveys.	**HOW:** ongoing, evidenced through practice. Monitor through practitioner evaluations (self and administrator).
MISSION STATEMENT: start writing down thoughts here.	

As you work through creating your mission statement, keep in mind that it will also guide your program's decisions and goals.

Introducing Vision and Mission Changes to Families

The Vision and Mission statement should reflect what family engagement will look like in your program, as in the examples. Once the Vision and Mission statements have been created, the introduction of the family engagement policy can be drafted. It should include a definition of engagement and why it is essential. Remember that you are addressing the *who, what, where, when, why, and how* questions for *each policy*. The first page of your policy statement could look something like the following example. I have emphasized how each question is addressed concerning the family engagement principles.

Hands On Learning Preschool

Family Engagement Policy

Our Vision

Hands On Learning Preschool: where children, families, and educators grow and learn together through play every day!

Our Mission

Hands On Learning Preschool exists to provide children and their families with stimulating and developmentally appropriate experiences. These experiences support the physical, intellectual, linguistic, and emotional/social domains of growth and learning. Our teachers provide these experiences daily in a natural environment, helping children's natural desire and curiosity to explore the world around them. We consider the child's family, both immediate and extended, vital to the learning process. We strive to meet all families where they are in their ability to engage through various play-based experiences.

In these daily experiences, children spend most of their day exploring specific interest areas – Creative Art, Math, Blocks, Language/Literacy,

Science/Discovery, and Dramatic Play. Through these experiences, they learn the foundational skills needed for higher learning and critical thinking. We engage families in this process by providing information on developmental milestones, the state early learning guidelines, and supplemental activities completed at home in various ways. We will also connect families to learning experiences outside of our program. We ask families to provide us with information on their values, beliefs, and desires for their child's learning. In turn, we will provide various forms and means of communication to inform families of their child's growth and development. Families are encouraged to partner with their child's teachers, administrators, community members, and policymakers to fully support the growth and development process.

Introduction to the Hands On Learning Family Engagement Policy

Our program believes family engagement is an essential piece of the learning process because we support the family as the child's first and primary teacher. Our goal is to involve all family members as they are able and in a manner that is comfortable to them. Ways you can engage with us include the following:

- Communicating with your child's caregivers regularly via *(list the opportunities you will include here – this will be addressed further as you create the next piece of the policy)*
- Participating in any or all the specific events we have prepared for families:
  - Surveys.
  - Questionnaires.
  - Family Conferences.
  - Family Learning Activities.

Family engagement takes place in many different areas and is available all the time. Specifically, we will:

- Ask you to complete an intake survey within 2 weeks of enrollment that gives us information to better serve your child and you to meet their educational needs.

- Ask you to complete an Ages and Stages questionnaire (ASQ) to bridge what you see at home to what we see at school.
  - This allows for better curriculum planning for your child and helps us connect meaningful learning experiences at home.
  - These questionnaires will be sent home for completion 2 weeks before each family conference.
- Ask you to participate in family conferences as your schedule allows.
  - We will hold these conferences based on each family's needs for time and availability.
  - We have set aside three days throughout the school year that are specifically for these events and are available all day between the hours of ____ and ____.
  - Each family has 30 minutes of one-on-one with the caregivers, and your child will be an active participant.
  - There will be on-site childcare provided for siblings.
- Ask you to participate in family learning activities both in our program and in the community as you are able. There will be many opportunities throughout the year and they will be in a variety of formats. For example:
  - We will have theme-based take-home activity bags that you and your child can explore together as they relate to our current topics of study. There will also be ideas included in each theme/topic's introduction letter for activities to do at home.
  - Periodically throughout the school year (one per quarter), we will hold Family Learning Nights. The first half of the evening will be for family education (free childcare is offered). The second half will include activities for you and your child to do together. We will provide dinner for the whole family at these events for $10 per family.
  - Participate in the local health and wellness fair by presenting a make and take activity for the children who attend.
- We will keep you informed of opportunities to work within our program:
  - Family Advisory Council
  - Advocacy Nights

You can expect to see these invitations to participate through the communications and opportunities for engagement as described previously, as well as the individual classroom blogs, photos, newsletters, and our Facebook page. Our doors are always open to you, and we look forward to hearing your ideas of how you would like to share your time and talent with us. We want to talk with you at drop-off and pick-up times and via text, email, or appointments outside of our regular opportunities. Please download the preschool app (*name of the app*) to learn more about how we can all partner together for your child's success.

From the creation of the Vision and Mission Statements, the introduction to the family engagement policy provides a more detailed outline for your policy's development. You have provided the first *invitation* for families to engage in partnership with the program. Compare what has been presented in this chapter to the example "Open Door Policy." These two statements and outline have gone well past telling families "We want you to know you are welcome here any time." Think about this from the family perspective and, of course, the *Field of Dreams* analogy from Chapter 1 – we must first build it. In doing so, we have invited them to come. I want to state again that it takes time and patience and a lot of trial and error. You will make changes and revisions as you go. More importantly, keep in mind that you likely will not get 100% engagement in 100% of the policies you implement. However, when you start with the vision that advises families "we are all in this together," you will see those numbers rise.

Whether you are creating new Vision and Mission statements or already have these in place, use the following worksheets to brainstorm ideas and adjust them to meet family engagement components. Remember to include the information in the process from the previous chapters to ensure you are addressing all families you serve, understanding their needs, and setting the foundation for the next step, which is building relationships.

Worksheet 1: Vision and Mission Statement Creation

Family Handbook Vision Statement Include all the details needed for families to know what your vision is for them and their child.	**Practitioner Handbook Vision Statement** Include all the details needed for program employees to know how to support the vision.
WHY:	**WHY:**
WHO:	**WHO:**
WHAT:	**WHAT:**
WHERE:	**WHERE:**
WHEN:	**WHEN:**
HOW:	**HOW:**
VISION STATEMENT:	

Parent Handbook Mission Statement Include all the details needed for families to know what your mission is for them and their child.	Practitioner Handbook Vision Statement Include all the details needed for program employees to know how to support the mission.
WHY:	WHY:
WHO:	WHO:
WHAT:	WHAT:
WHERE:	WHERE:
WHEN:	WHEN:
HOW:	HOW:
MISSION STATEMENT:	

References

Bruno, H. E. (2008). *Leading on purpose: Emotionally intelligent early childhood administration.* New York, NY: McGraw-Hill.

Carter, M., & Curtis, D. (2010). *The visionary director: A handbook for dreaming, organizing, and improvising in your center.* St. Paul, MN: Redleaf Press.

Goffin, S. G., & Washington, V. (2007). *Ready or not: Leadership choices in early care and education.* New York, NY: Teacher's College Press.

National Association for the Education of Young Children. (2010). *Engaging diverse families project.* Retrieved from www.naeyc.org/familyengagement/about

5 It All Starts With Relationships

In the previous chapter, you began laying the foundation of your engagement policy – congratulations! In this chapter, you will apply the next level of understanding – building *relationships* with the families you serve. In the mission statement, I laid the foundation by letting families know they *are encouraged to partner with their child's teachers, administrators, community members, and policymakers to fully support the growth and development process*. Now, it is time to define how it will be accomplished.

To begin this process, it is important to know why building relationships is important. In Chapters 1 and 2, the foundational background for family engagement focused on the fact that families are their child's first teacher and that the home is their first educational program. As such, families are already invested in promoting their child's development, learning, and overall wellness. Second, we are tasked with including the family in the planning of curriculum and assessment. Last, practitioners must actively engage families as partners to accomplish these tasks. The relationships must also be *nurtured*.

To nurture these relationships, you must revisit the types of families you serve and identify the essential information you need to build individual relationships. The family intake survey (see Appendix B) will give you a great start to knowing and understanding the families in your program. In this survey, ask families what they want and what they need. For example, according to Gross and O'Neil-Hart (2017, as cited in Koralek et al., 2019), forty percent of people in the millennial generation are parents. In their study of millennial families, they found that:

- One-third of these families follow traditional gender roles and share responsibilities equally.

- One-third want to share responsibilities equally; however, the female parent primarily takes on the task of primary caregiver and child-rearing.
- *45% of all millennial moms are staying home with their children!*
- Millennial parents are more accepting of non-gender-conforming clothing, toys, and experiences.
- Millennial dads believe involvement with their children is a masculine trait.
- 75% continue to pursue their personal goals after having children.
- These families know about child development but may have information overload from the abundance of information available through the internet and social media.
    - 86% of millennial dads use YouTube for key parenting information such as meal preparations or using products.
    - 82% of these dads watch videos on YouTube related to general or pop-culture news to connect with their children.
- *61% of millennial parents believe families can never be too involved* (Chart 2, Chapter 2).

Further, Millennial and Gen X families interviewed (Riser, 2018, as cited in Koralek et al., 2019) stated that:

- They are proud of raising children but recognize there are challenges. 90% said parenting was their "greatest joy", but 70% stated it was their biggest challenge.
- They need and want information and support. 80% stated that they work hard to be better parents, and if they knew more about parenting, they would apply it. Over half of these families stated that they are not getting the support they need to cope with stress.
- Practitioners need to make connections with significant male family caregivers – not just dads but uncles, grandfathers, and even great-grandfathers – who want to be involved.
- Families cannot find resources or information they *trust*. They do not trust information that comes from people who do not know their situation or their child.

- Millennial and Gen X families *want to know about:*
  - Social/emotional development.
  - Brain development.
  - Developmental milestones.
  - Effective discipline strategies.
  - Help understanding and being patient with their children.

Understanding these cultural and social values and identifying barriers to engagement must be taken into consideration. Generally, when we think about obstacles, we tend to think first about the time commitment, then perhaps financial constraints. However, often families will not engage because they believe their goals differ from those of the practitioner's (Demircan & Erden, 2015; Goodall & Montgomery, 2014; Morrison, Storey, & Zhang, 2015). Knowing the information in the previous list and doing your own research on the families you serve is vital to building relationships. As a practitioner, do not assume that family members are not interested in or unwilling to engage – the desire may be there, but the barriers seem insurmountable.

When quality engagement practices are employed, families understand they are welcomed and valued as partners in reciprocal relationships. To address what is known, practitioners should recognize and address the beliefs and values of the families served and help address the challenges. A trusting relationship with families can be built through first hearing and supporting their needs and wants, then connecting them to appropriate and useful research-based resources. Encouraging and inviting all family members to become part of the relationship further recognizes them as the child's primary caregivers and educators.

Effective Strategies for Relationship Building

Exactly when and where do these relationships start? From the beginning! Not only must you learn about your families, but you must also allow them to get to know you! Think back to your Vision and Mission Statements – do you practice these daily? What are the first messages families get about your program?

Your initial verbal contact is likely over the phone – what is your phone presence? Are phone calls answered promptly, and are they professional? I have called so many centers where they absolutely were not handled appropriately.

It All Starts With Relationships

Practitioners often answer the phone in a harried voice, sounding as though they have neither the time nor the patience to deal with who is on the other end. Identify and implement a good phone protocol, as you never know who is on the other end. What is your conversation like with prospective families? It is important to be consistent with how these are handled. Remember that the keyword in family engagement is *invite* – invite the families to your program. The first phone conversation will set the tone for relationship building.

Information is key, and first impressions are a good indicator of the type of relationships you will form with families. Once you have spoken with them on the phone, lead them to more information. Offer to email, mail, or locate information on your Vision and Mission statements. If you do not have a web presence, think about creating one. Programs such as GoDaddy™ or Wix are user friendly and can be set up quickly. Develop a Facebook Business page in addition to a website as a good starting place to inform future (and current) families about your program. Provide a photo gallery (only with photo releases from current families) to let them "see" what you do. Ultimately, though, the goal is to get them into your program and to experience what you have to offer.

The next impression a family has is when they pull into your parking lot before you meet them at the door (and, whenever possible, you should meet them at the door). What your curb appeal says about your program is very meaningful. If it is unorganized and chaotic, this is how they will view your overall program, and they will approach cautiously with negative thoughts. Think about providing VIP parking spaces for visiting/new families that are close to the door. Post a sign that can be changed to put the family's name on it (when you know they are coming) or one that says, "Reserved for Prospective Families". One space with a very important message – "they value me and my family."

A welcoming environment should meet the needs of the family. Families should enter a visually pleasing reception area that is conducive to both children and adults. For both children and adults, the reception area should be pleasing to the five senses. In my reception area, I had two separate areas, one for children with a child-sized table and chairs, a soft mat, and throw pillows on the floor. I had a small shelf that held books, puzzles, and other materials that represented all ages and the types of activities found in the classrooms. There was also a fish tank that was at the right height for both child and adult viewing. For adults, I had two adult-sized, comfortable chairs, a side table with a lamp (no harsh overhead lighting), and parent resource materials, including copies of parenting magazines they could take home. Many magazine publishers will provide these to you for free, hoping families will purchase a subscription. I also provided a snack cart with coffee for adults, small bottles of water, juice boxes, and healthy snacks (available for all families, not just prospective ones). The décor was natural woods and live, nontoxic greenery (often planted by the children during study units). On the adult side, one wall had a photo gallery and a short bio of all practitioners in my program. On the other wall, I rotated art pieces created by the children. Each piece was labeled with the child's first name, the child's description of his/her piece, the child's age and classroom, and the date it was completed. The children's walls included a small mural of flowers, butterflies, and kids. Finally, we had a tv monitor mounted in a corner that presented snapshots from each classroom in real time. Think about the messages sent to not only the family but any visitor entering your program. The bottom line for creating this welcoming environment was to let families and children know clearly how much we value *them*. What better way to begin a relationship? Take a moment and sketch out your current reception area – regardless of size, think about how you can create a welcoming area that lets families know they are important to you. Use the blank page that follows to dream and create. My area described previously was all in just a 200 square-foot space.

When you greet the family, they have already received an impression of what to expect. Families want to know that you are interested in them and their child. If the child is present, greet him or her first. Then greet the family, welcome them to your program, and invite them to your office or a quiet area dedicated to family conferences. In both my office and our family resource room, I again had a child-sized table and chairs with activities for the child to do while I talked to the family. This supported the message that I cared about them and allowed us to have a good conversation. Every so often, I would stop and ask the child a question or two about them as well, depending on their age, of course. If I was enrolling an infant, I asked if I could hold the child – again, demonstrating to the family that I cared for them and their child. In that meeting, I provided each family with our PIP – Parent Information Packet. This was a two-pocket folder (the ones you can buy very inexpensively during back-to-school sales) that held copies of our family handbook and the intake forms for enrollment. It also held a free book for them to keep for their child, as well as pamphlets and brochures on resources from the community. This was the second layer of relationship building.

The final layer of relationship building was the parent tour. Regardless of the age of the child, the family toured the entire building and outdoor spaces.

I tried to manage all parent tours, however, in case I was not available, the assistant director or one of the head teachers was trained to do them. Yes, I said trained. Because I want to build relationships with families and all practitioners, I created a specific protocol for parent tours. One specific piece of the tour was to introduce the family to all teachers and all the children. When I opened the door to each classroom, I would say, "Hello friends! This is Jane and Jon Doe and their little boy Jack. Can you all say hello?" Then I would introduce the teachers in the room who, at a minimum, would greet them verbally and welcome them to their room. If time or the situation permitted, they could share a bit about what was happening at that moment with the children (center exploration, circle, snack – whatever they were doing at the moment). I never informed my practitioners of planned family tours, and most of them were spur of the moment. They were always prepared and aware a family could come in at any time – and it always showed. There were hectic moments of course – we are talking about preschoolers! When that happened, they responded to the touring family with something like "Our friends are very excited today, as you can tell" or "As you can see the weather has us all a bit antsy." This tells the family that a) this is normal for preschoolers, and b) we have this under control. These stops on our tour helped build relationships by letting the family know "we are all in this together." The family could be assured that, even on the worst days, our practitioners were in control and still were able to smile through it all.

Once the tour was completed, the family and I returned to the same area we started and reviewed the family handbook, policies, and procedures. In this meeting, there is an exchange of information to learn about the family as much as possible. Using the family intake survey (Appendix A), I asked some informal questions and wrote down some of the answers in a notebook that was specifically for family tours. I then invited them to ask me questions, which I also recorded. Doing so gave me insight into not only this family's needs and wants but into those of other families. If the child enrolled, these notes then went into the family's file. The final step in this process was providing each family with a free day of care in our program. They made an appointment (they chose the day; we gave an appointment card so we could ensure ratio), and the child would come and spend the day with us. I ended each meeting by thanking them for coming, telling them how much I enjoyed meeting them and their child, thanking the child for visiting me, and reminding them to review their materials, jot down any further questions, and not to hesitate to call or come back. It is all about building a relationship – from the start.

How are all these items crucial for *relationships?* The *messages* behind each action. From the moment a family has set foot in your facility, you have initiated a relationship. As a reminder, these relationships are *critical* in all the family engagement principles. Specifically, NAEYC's principle 3 indicates (2010) that practitioners need to engage families in truly reciprocal ways. *Reciprocal relationships* are defined as those in which 2 parties agree to do something similar for each other and/or allow each other the same rights regarding the relationship's roles and functions (www.merriam-webster.com/dictionary/reciprocal#learn-more). When applied to family engagement, it ensures that both parties are working together to support the child's education. While practitioners are tasked with respecting the family as the child's first teacher, it is important to note how much time children spend in the care of someone outside the home. For example, there are 168 hours in a week (7 days times 24 hours). If we assume the average of 8 hours per day for sleep, that leaves 112 waking hours for interactions with the child. If the child is enrolled in your program 45 hours per week, that leaves 67 hours spent with family, not including any time spent with other caregivers or family members outside of program enrollment. The balance of time the child spends with the family is only slightly more than that spent with the practitioners. Thus, developing these relationships is imperative to keep everyone informed about the child's progress – practitioners need to know what happens at home, and families need to know what happens in the program. It is a continuous cycle that must be supported through intentionally planned activities and communication strategies, which will be discussed as the next building block in Chapter 6.

As you begin to write your own policy of relationship building, remember the questions from Chapter 3 and how each should be addressed in your program. Knight-McKenna and Hollingsworth (2016) identified principles that foster strengths-based partnerships with families. Practitioners and families need to (a) embrace an expanded definition of the family, (b) make concerted efforts to reach out to families, (c) learn about each family's background and perspectives, (d) implement and practice effective communication strategies, (e) withhold assumptions and judgments, (f) engage in identifying family strengths, (g) view each other as equals, (h) support aspirations of the program and the family, (i) engage in identifying common goals, (j) support the ability for and level of engagement, (k) connect to community resources, and (l) employ patience and persistence, which, in turn, develops trust over time. Your policies will also evolve over time and are supported through *repeated interactions* between practitioners and family members. When implemented, these will lead to a deeper understanding of the partnership and the foundation to shared responsibility for the child's well-being (Knight-McKenna & Hollingsworth, 2016). There must be a balance between practitioner expectations and family flexibility to provide optimal engagement and relationship-building experiences (Matthews & Rix, 2013). Employing the principles outlined previously assists practitioners to integrate family knowledge into the curriculum and activities within the classroom.

As you jot your ideas on the worksheet, remember:

- Who are the members of the relationship (the family members, the educators, and the child)?
- What is the purpose of the relationship?
- Where are these relationships formed and supported?
- Why are they needed? The answer to this question will likely connect back to your vision/mission and the information included in the foundational knowledge from previous chapters.
- When can these relationships be formed and supported?
- Most importantly, how will the relationships develop and be nurtured?

While I have provided examples from my own program, you must develop what is right for your families and your program. Further examples of activities that can support the development of intentional, reciprocal relationships include some of the following:

- Planning activities for or inviting families on the waiting list to events you have already planned – what a positive message this sends to families who have not started your program yet!
- First impressions – curb appeal (outside appearances matter), reception area designed around both adults and children, designated parking for first-time families/visitors, intentional parent tours (remember the five senses).
- Information packets for new neighborhood residents – connect with realtor agencies.
- Intake meetings to discuss the philosophy of your program.
- Creating a website and/or Facebook page where practitioners and families can interact.

It All Starts With Relationships

- Providing a family resource room.
- Creating family events that include learning with the children.
- Provide family events without children (provide care services).
- Highlight a "Family of the Week" in your newsletter, online, and other materials.
- Provide parenting workshops based on topics of interest from the family.
- Use suggestion boxes or surveys to gather issues and areas that might need improvement.
- After the intake survey, offer other periodic surveys that ask families how they feel about your program.
- Connect families to webinars on child development.
- Provide your own family education nights.
- Provide family "meet and greet" activities at different times of the day and throughout the year.

It is also essential to think about your initial meetings and what you know about the families you serve – thinking further about the information about Gen X and Millennial families in this chapter and the information you identified about your families in Chapter 3.

- What current issues are families facing?
- Are there educator assumptions (good or not so good) regarding families?
- Do your families feel empowered and honored? (If so, how? If not, how can you change it?)

Finally, remember the concepts needed to build the comprehensive system of engagement. *Invite* the families to help in not only providing suggestions for these activities but also with the planning and implementation. In the end, families want to know that their child is in good hands, that they have the information they need about their child's time in the program, and that they have ideas and support to work with their child at home. The at-home activities will be further outlined in Chapter 7. Before you can successfully create and implement these, the relationship-building block must be put into place.

Once again, it is your turn! Use the outline on the following page to start writing your ideas and thoughts about how you will invite your families to form reciprocal relationships.

Worksheet 2: Program/Family/Community Relationships – Policy

Parent Handbook	Educator Handbook
WHY:	**WHY:**
WHO:	**WHO:**
WHAT:	**WHAT**
WHERE:	**WHERE:**
WHEN:	**WHEN:**
HOW:	**HOW:**

References

Demircan, Ö., & Erden, F. T. (2015). Parental involvement and developmentally appropriate practices: A comparison of parent and teacher beliefs. *Early Child Development and Care, 185*, 209–225. https://doi.org/10.1080/03004430.2014.919493

Goodall, J., & Montgomery, C. (2014). Parental involvement to parental engagement: A continuum. *Educational Review, 66*, 399–410. https://doi.org/10.1080.00131911.2013.781576

Knight-McKenna, M., & Hollingsworth, H. L. (2016). Fostering family – Teacher partnerships: Principles in practice. *Childhood Education, 92*, 383–390. https://doi.org/10.1080/00094056.2016.1226113

Koralek, D., Nemeth, K., & Ramsey, K. (2019). *Families & educators together: Building great relationships that support young children*. Washington, DC: NAEYC.

Matthews, A., & Rix, J. (2013). Early intervention: Parental involvement, child agency, and participation in creative play. *Early Years: An International Research Journal, 33*, 239–251. https://doi.org/10.1080/09575146.2013.766151

Morrison, J. W., Storey, P., & Zhang, C. (2015). Accessible family involvement in early childhood programs. *Dimensions of Early Childhood, 39*(3), 33–38. Retrieved from www.southernearlychildhood.org/upload/pdf/Accessible_Family_Involvement_in_Early_Childhood_Programs_by_Johnetta_W__Morrison_Pamela_Storey_and_Chenyi_Zhang.pdf

National Association for the Education of Young Children. (2010). *Engaging diverse families project*. Retrieved from www.naeyc.org/familyengagement/about

Effective Communication Practices and Strategies

Now that you have established policies regarding reciprocal relationships with families, it is important to support those relationships through intentional communication policies. In my research, most practitioners felt that their communication strategies and formats were "sufficient," but families did not appear to "pay attention" to them. In this portion of the policy, you will look at how to address this challenging issue and *engage* the family in communication practices.

The first aspect to address is, as with the example from my research, that of *perspective*. In the previous chapters, you learned about meeting families "where they are". To do so, you identified their characteristics, values, beliefs, and goals. It is equally important to understand their perspective, keeping in mind our own as well. To understand perspective, complete this quick exercise.

> *Reflect on your own qualities, characteristics, values, and beliefs. Circle the word below that BEST describes you:*
> *Optimistic*
> *Imaginative*
> *Idealistic*
> *Self-confident*
> *Team Player*
> *Now reflect on why this word best describes you, and write about it here:*
>
> *Last, look at how others might perceive you based on your word:*
> *Optimistic – others may see you as impractical*

Effective Communication Practices

Imaginative – others may view you as a dreamer with no goals
Idealistic – you are a wishful thinker
Self-confident – others may see you as arrogant
Team Player – you are dependent on others to do your work

Figure 6.1 Perceptions Girl in Mirror

Kathryn E. McKay

Surprised at the outcome? While many of these are admirable qualities, others may view them as unfavorable regardless of perspective. In the previous example, where practitioners felt families "did not pay attention" – how might this be perceived differently? Families have limited time and busy schedules, remember? Maybe they forgot, or, worse, possibly due to language barriers, they did not understand. Are there families who will ignore communication efforts? Absolutely. Are there ways in which practitioners can creatively fine-tune their strategies to engage those families? Absolutely. Before you think about the first step in creating better communication strategies, it is essential to know what the research says about how it works in the family engagement paradigm.

Why Are Communication Strategies Important?

Families often identify the lack of communication or poor communication as a barrier in developing engagement relationships (Demircan & Erden, 2015). Research indicates that the *quality* and *quantity* of communication with families predict their engagement level. It should also be considered an integral aspect of *developing relationships* between family members and practitioners (Epstein, 2001; Nitecki, 2015; Sánchez & Walsh, 2017; Tran, 2014). Communication and relationships are interrelated – one is mutually dependent on the other. When communication is two-way, ongoing, consistent, and clear, families develop a higher interest in what the program is doing. They are also more likely to participate in other aspects of the program, improving overall engagement relationships (Baker, Wise, Kelley, & Skiba, 2016; Epstein, 2001). Communication is an important foundation in all relationships but is especially important in the relationship between family and education practitioners and must be built on a foundation of mutual trust and respect (Nitecki, 2015).

Communication should be ongoing, timely, and continuous. Two-way, collaborative communication recognizes the need for both program- and family-initiated communication (Epstein, 2001; NAEYC, 2010). The information shared should relate to the program's practices, events, family development and support, and community services and events. Communication strategies should focus on adding to each member's knowledge, exchanging ideas, and developing a plan for action, such as in the decision-making and goal-setting process (Chapters 8 and 9). Communication formats should include ways for this exchange of knowledge and idea-sharing to occur. Information collected in this process is then used to support curriculum in the program, activities for learning at home, and activities for learning in the community.

All forms of communication should be provided in different languages and delivery format to accommodate the diverse needs of families, which can be identified through ongoing feedback on family preferences of communication format and style (Baker et al., 2016; Nitecki, 2015; Sánchez &Walsh, 2017; Tran, 2014). The most common example of family communication is the parent conference. These are generally held at least once a year and include a discussion (usually brief) on the child's progress and behavior. These infrequent conferences, however, cannot take the place of valuable information that is gained from ongoing conversations between practitioners and families that occur during drop-off and pick-up times or program activities and events. It is the in-between times where communication policy should be focused. Regular, more brief forms of communication such as written notes, memos, phone calls, texts, newsletters, and the like should be provided. Each communication format should be personal and one-on-one whenever possible.

Everyone benefits when communication is emphasized as important in the program (Epstein, 2001). For children, open communication creates an awareness of their own progress and actions they may need to make to progress in their own learning. Children also become aware of the program's rules, policies, and procedures and their responsibility to follow them. High-quality communication allows practitioners to develop an increased awareness and understanding of diversity in each family and to provide for individual planning for the children in their care (Baker et al., 2016; Calzada et al., 2015; Epstein, 2001). Families benefit by knowing and understanding more about child growth and development and using that information to fully support their child. Positive communication strategies yield positive results for everyone in the partnership. When policies and procedures are clearly outlined from the beginning, families understand what is expected of them and what they can expect from the program (Epstein, 2001).

How to Improve Communication Strategies

Ideally, policies for appropriate communication strategies should be developed before opening a program for services, established firmly in the family policies' content. This does not mean that what is currently in place cannot be modified or improved! It is crucial to understand that communication practices will evolve and change as family and societal changes occur (Nitecki, 2015; Sánchez & Walsh, 2017). For example, in my program, communication was mostly written, as we were just on the cusp of cell phones and texting. Today there are many technology applications for use in communication between practitioners and family members. Many programs have their own websites, blogs, and Facebook pages. Technology has changed our communication abilities!

Regardless of format, all communication should envelop these principles, as outlined by Borruel (2016):

- Emphasis should be placed on professionalism. Practitioners must know and practice appropriate oral and verbal communication skills to ensure quality and readability.
- Remember the relationship.
- Ensure that communication is positive. They hear the "bad" all the time. Focus on the positive using the sandwich technique – positive/negative/positive.
- Keep it personable – warm and friendly, even if it is not merited.
- Be proactive. Practitioners should initiate (invite) conversations. Encourage families to do the same (reciprocal).
- Demonstrate your passion for what you do. Let families know that this is your passion, and you are proud of it. Communicate how much you want to make a difference in the field and especially in their child's life.
- Communicate problems with tact and skill and maintain confidentiality. Relate issues to the facts such as the developmental domains and child development knowledge and research, or your state early learning standards/guidelines.
- Provide the basic daily information parents need to know, supplemented with the fun stuff.

- Always uphold the philosophy of the program (Vision and Mission statements).

Communication Strategies

Initial Communications

Developing intentional strategies to build relationships, such as those outlined in Chapter 5, will also build the foundation for two-way communication between the family and practitioners. Creating a welcoming environment, providing materials, using an intake survey, and getting to know each family sets the stage for future communications. In the PIP (parent information packet), I provided copies of the forms used for all written communications and a copy of the current newsletter. If you have a Facebook page and/or website, provide them the information needed to log in and find information. If you use an early childhood app for smartphones, be sure to provide information on how it can be accessed and how it will be used for communication.

Parent Introduction Boards

A great way to introduce new families to everyone is to create a space that displays family information. Instead of the old "Me and My Family" projects sent home to families, invite them to share their values, beliefs, culture, hobbies, and other information on a display board (I provided the boards). These were hung in our commons area (the area that led to all classrooms) and not only taught us about the family, but families learned about and developed relationships with each other. The premise behind this activity is that these were great conversation starters. Often, families would want to add to them throughout the year, such as when a new sibling was born or they had a new adventure or adopted a new pet.

Family Information Boards

Each classroom had a bulletin board outside of their door that contained important information that families needed to know about their child's room and activities. The board was where the menu, the daily schedule, a copy of the weekly or monthly lesson plans, notices of events, and important reminders were placed. Pocket folders held printed copies of the classroom and program newsletters. Other pieces of information for these boards include emergency plans and procedures, allergy charts (concerning privacy), copies of articles practitioners want to share with families, policy reminders, announcements, and the "What Happened in our Room Today" sheets discussed in the next section.

Written/Digital Communications

Each classroom had regular written communication with families about their child's day – the regular information about eating, sleeping, and toileting throughout the day. Additionally, at the end of each day, a "What Happened in our Room Today" sheet was posted with pictures and short descriptions of the educational activities of the day. At the end of the week, a documentation board was created (new photos and descriptions) to further highlight the activities the children enjoyed. Each classroom sent home a monthly newsletter that was specific to their classroom. I sent home a monthly program newsletter that included articles on child development topics and overall program news and events.

Family Conferences

The parent/family conference gives everyone, including the child, an opportunity to discuss and understand educational progress and address any issues. In my program, the first piece of the family conference included the family filling out an Ages and Stages Questionnaire (ASQ®) on their child, based on their experiences at home. During the conference, the child had a special form they filled out to share their learning with the family (see Appendix C). The form had a box for each question, and the child could draw and dictate their answers to the following:

- I am great at:
- I need help with:
- I want to learn more about:

Effective Communication Practices

The family also filled out a similar form that asked these questions (see Appendix C):

- We think our child does well with:
- We feel our child needs help with:
- We have the following questions about our child's progress:

Practitioners provided the following information collected in the time between conferences:

- Portfolio/work samples.
- Developmental checklists.
- Anecdotal notes.
- Photo and/or video documentation.
- Screening instruments (if used).

Together, the family and the practitioners shared information and knowledge to support the child's developmental progress. It is in these conferences that families can participate in the decision-making and goal-setting process, which will be addressed further in Chapter 8.

As you start thinking about how to develop strategies for communicating with families and creating this portion of your policy, consider how you might implement some of the following ideas.

- Family and practitioner communication opportunities.
- Engaging in short, two-way conversations during drop-off and pick-up times.
  - For families who may not be able to do so, consider having a communication notebook located in or on each child's cubby for back-and-forth communication.
- Use the communication preference survey (Appendix A) to determine how and when to communicate with individual families (meet them where they are).
- Use the communication tracker (Appendix A) to reflect on past communication experiences and track engagement.

Effective Communication Practices

- Consider providing one of the new smartphone apps for programs:
    - SeeSaw – https://web.seesaw.me/.
    - Tadpoles – www.tadpoles.com/.
    - Brightwheel – https://mybrightwheel.com/.
    - Storypark – www.storypark.com/.
    - Procare Solutions – www.procaresoftware.com/child-care-app/.
- Create a Facebook Business Page that can include:
    - Blogs.
    - Upload of newsletters and other communications.
    - Photos and live videos.
    - Access to important documents for prospective and current families.
- Create a program website that can coordinate in more detail with your Facebook page and other social media.
- Newsletters provided at regular intervals (first of each month, for example: see Appendix C).
    - Consistent in format.
    - Provided in different formats.
    - Provided in different languages.
- Use phone calls for GOOD information! "Today, your child did the most amazing thing!"
- Handwritten notes sent home that focus on the GOOD, not only the negatives. These can be more meaningful in our technological world! (See Appendix C.)
- Send e-mails that update, invite, share, and ask for information in return.
- Family resource bulletin boards (and/or whiteboards for information changes).
    - Provide a bulletin board that is dedicated to community resources, events, and agencies.
- Specific forms/formats for specific issues:
    - Daily notes that inform families of general care issues.
    - Incident and accident reports.
- Family-to-family communication opportunities.
    - Family socializing events.
    - Family gathering place.

- Family/educator/community communications
  - Op-Ed, articles in local papers.
  - Blogs.

There is no single communication strategy or format that should be relied upon as a standalone practice. Instead, practitioners should keep in mind using at least three different methods in three different types of delivery format for each type of communication. For example, have the program's newsletter available in paper, text, and email format. Remember, you can now use computer programs such as Google Translate to create communication in families' native languages.

Communication in any form has challenges to be addressed to fully support and involve all families. Take into consideration family reading levels, and keep written forms to a minimum and offer oral communication when possible. When creating communication pieces, practitioners must know and practice appropriate oral and verbal communication skills to ensure quality, readability, and the family's comfort level. Finally, practitioners must also be prepared for and skilled in how to deal with family members who may become hostile or indifferent using the simple rules of general communication: active listening, positive phrasing, and constructive feedback and remembering to keep emotions in check (Mahmood, 2013; Sherwood & Nind, 2014).

Keeping in mind that communication strategies and relationships are both reciprocal and interrelated, it is that time again! Use the worksheet on the next page to start forming your communication policy.

Effective Communication Practices

Worksheet 3: Communication – Policy

Parent Handbook	Educator Handbook
WHY:	WHY:
WHO:	WHO:
WHAT:	WHAT
WHERE:	WHERE:
WHEN:	WHEN:
HOW:	HOW:

References

Baker, T. L., Wise, J., Kelley, G., & Skiba, R. J. (2016). Identifying barriers: Creating solutions to improve family engagement. *School Community Journal, 26,* 161–184. Retrieved from https://files.eric.ed.gov/fulltext/EJ1124003.pdf

Borruel, T. W. (2016). The ten p's of parent communication. In *The art of leadership: Engaging families in early childhood organizations* (pp. 56–59). Lincoln, NE: Exchange Press.

Calzada, E. J., Huang, K., Hernandez, M., Soriano, E., Acra, C. F., Dawson-McClure, S., & Brotman, L. (2015). Family and teacher characteristics as predictors of parent involvement in education during early childhood among Afro-Caribbean and Latino immigrant families. *Urban Education, 50,* 870–896. https://doi.org/10.1177/0042085914534862

Demircan, Ö., & Erden, F. T. (2015). Parental involvement and developmentally appropriate practices: A comparison of parent and teacher beliefs. *Early Child Development and Care, 185,* 209–225. https://doi.org/10.1080/03004430.2014.919493

Epstein, J. (2001). *School, family, and community partnerships: Preparing educators and improving schools.* Boulder, CO: Westview Press.

Mahmood, S. (2013). First-year preschool and kindergarten teachers: Challenges of working with parents. *School Community Journal, 23*(2), 55–85. Retrieved from https://files.eric.ed.gov/fulltext/EJ1028824.pdf

National Association for the Education of Young Children. (2010). *Engaging diverse families project.* Retrieved from www.naeyc.org/familyengagement/about

Nitecki, E. (2015). Integrated school-family partnerships in preschool: Building quality involvement through multidimensional relationships. *School Community Journal, 25,* 195–219. Retrieved from https://files.eric.ed.gov/fulltext/EJ1085725.pdf

Sánchez, C., & Walsh, B. (2017). Meeting national expectations for partnering with families. *Dimensions of Early Childhood, 45*(2), 20–28. Retrieved from www.southernearlychildhood.org/page.php?purl=seca_publications

Sherwood, G., & Nind, M. A. (2014). Parents' experiences of support: Co-constructing their stories. *International Journal of Early Years Education*, *22*, 457–470. https://doi.org/10.1080/09669760.2014.970520

Tran, Y. (2014). Addressing reciprocity between families and schools: Why these bridges are instrumental for students' academic success. *Improving Schools*, *17*, 18–29. https://doi.org /10.1177/1365480213515296

# Extending Learning in the Home and Community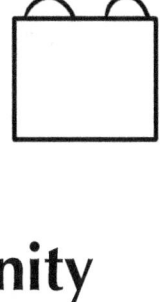

Previously, you learned how to develop relationships with the family and support those relationships through communication strategies. Strategies for communication included daily interactions within the family context. In these practices, children learn social and educational expectations. You also learned that the relationship between the family and the child is an essential part of family engagement practices. In this chapter, the need for practitioners to support the family as a valuable resource in the child's learning process is examined. The goal of this policy is to connect learning experiences among the home, the program, and the community.

Connecting Learning at Home to Family Engagement

Once reciprocal relationships and communication practices with families have been developed, the information collected can be used to support families in providing educational experiences outside of the program. The fourth principle outlined by NAEYC (2010) emphasizes the practitioner's need to provide learning activities in the home. Practitioners are also encouraged to connect families to these opportunities in the community.

Learning at home was supported throughout the foundational frameworks of Epstein (2001); Halgunseth, Petereson, Stark, and Moodie (2009); and Weiss, Caspe, and Lopez (2006). Learning opportunities in the home and community are directly connected to reciprocal relationships and effective communication strategies. When these components are in place, families and practitioners work together to create at-home activities to enhance the family's ability to support their child's education (Demircan & Erden, 2015; Halgunseth et al., 2009; Murray, McFarland-Piazza, & Harrison, 2015).

Learning at home begins with the family's belief that learning is essential. While the families believe they are capable, they may lack the confidence to provide learning opportunities within the home (Calzada et al., 2015; Goodall & Montgomery, 2014). Practitioners should view the family as co-constructors of learning, even though family members may doubt their knowledge and abilities (Brown, Knoche, Edwards, & Sheridan, 2009; Nitecki, 2015; Summer & Summer, 2014). Practitioners can support family members in this endeavor by suggesting ways to establish an environment at home that supports learning. Attention should be focused on making a connection between home and the program specifically to support academic learning, by providing information for the family about the current curriculum content (Epstein, 2001; McWayne, Melzi, Schick, Kennedy, & Mundt, 2013). When families can support learning experiences in the home, they model expectations for the child's attitude toward education (McWayne et al., 2013). When the family is viewed as an equal partner to the child's educator, an understanding is developed that learning occurs in a variety of places, not just the educational setting (Epstein, 2001; Schaub, 2015; Share & Kerrins, 2013; Sy, Gottfried, & Gottfried, 2013).

Through knowledge gained from relationship and communication efforts, practitioners can also support the family's home routines and guidance styles (Brown et al., 2009). Practitioners must look at how they can support the family in their role in children's lives. As mentioned in previous chapters, families have changed, and practitioners must embrace their composition and their roles in the child's life. The family now includes grandparents, guardians, foster parents, and older siblings. Understanding parents' and family members' role includes appreciating and accepting each family's attitudes, values, and practices in raising children. Additionally, they must intentionally plan when and how to deliver learning activities that will meet families' abilities and needs. It is important to remember the home is the first educational program children experience.

In Epstein's (2001) model, learning at home was directly supported by practitioners sending home activities that support the program's educational objectives. Providing the family with information on developmental milestones, early learning standards (state level), and other information helps them understand and connect learning to those objectives and goals. Families believe they can assist their children with educational activities, but they feel they do not have the proper support, materials, or information to do so (Demircan & Erden, 2015). Thus, when planning activities for at-home learning, practitioners should provide the materials and support needed for families to implement them effectively.

To further support learning at home, educational opportunities should also address child growth, learning, and development and developmentally appropriate practices. When families have the right information, they will be able to develop their own activities in the home. Offering opportunities to learn more in these areas can increase the family's confidence and ability to educate their child in the home. Informal educational opportunities can come from program-initiated home visits. Home visits, especially in the birth-through-three age group, allow practitioners to promote and demonstrate educational involvement with families. The original purpose of home visits was initially to give an educational boost to children who may be at risk (poverty, cultural background). Yet, visits promote these skills and support language, cognitive, and social development in all children, regardless of ethnic or economic background (Kellar-Guenther, Rosenberg, Block, & Robinson, 2014; Manz, Gernhart, Bracaliello, Pressimone, & Eisenberg, 2014; Morrison, Storey, & Zhang, 2015). Incorporating home visitation also supports the family as the child's primary educator by creating an academic focus at home (Manz et al., 2014). Such visits allow for conversations that provide information about the family outside of the child's educational goals and help build the mutual trust needed for communication, collaborative relationships, and shared decision making (Whyte & Karabon, 2016). When family education support is provided by the practitioners, family member behaviors, attitudes, beliefs, and engagement practices improve (Grindal et al., 2016; Ihmeideh & Oliemat, 2015).

The benefits of bridging learning between home and program are numerous. For children, the most important outcome is the continuous support and development of skills and knowledge (Summer & Summer, 2014). The child also begins to develop a love for learning, vital for continued academic success (Epstein, 2001; Ihmeideh & Oliemat, 2015). The child's self-concept is developed through this collaboration. The family members develop an appreciation and awareness of their child as a capable learner (Epstein, 2001). Families benefit by learning how to support and encourage the children in their learning and gaining an understanding of best practices for growth, development, and learning. Practitioners benefit by understanding how to plan curriculum for individual children, which directly correlates to the principles of developmentally appropriate practice guidelines (NAEYC, 2009). Practitioners also benefit by strengthening partnerships and respect for the diverse needs and situations of families. Learning at home supports respect for family time and their ability to participate in the child's education (Epstein, 2001). The challenges to supporting learning at home are like those in the other family engagement areas, such as time and language barriers. The goal for practitioners is to create a system in which they work with families collaboratively.

Strategies for Learning at Home

Children are more academically successful when the family is involved in educational experiences at home and within the program (McWayne et al., 2013). Thus, attention should be focused on connecting learning between the home and program. When the family is viewed as an equal partner to the child's educator, they understand that learning occurs in various places, not just the educational setting. Children learn best when support for education is present in the home combined with what is learned in the program.

The following is a list of examples of how learning at home can be implemented in connection with learning in the program.

- **Policy**
    - By now, this word is likely ingrained in your mind. Still, just as families need to know what you provide for engagement, they must also learn about the educational program. You touched on this in your Vision and Mission statements. Expand your policies to describe your curriculum methods fully. You can use the same principles outlined for your family engagement policies.
- **Inform**
    - As part of your efforts to engage families in the education process, provide them copies of the information they need to understand growth and development. Provide them – or help them obtain a copy of – developmental domains and milestones – my favorite is this book:

- Petty, K. (2016). *Developmental milestones of young children* (Rev. ed.). St. Paul, MN: Redleaf Press.
- Provide families with access to your state's:
  - Licensing regulations.
  - Early learning guidelines and standards.
    - To find your State's ELG's use this website: https://childcareta.acf.hhs.gov/resource/state-early-learning-standards-and-guidelines.
- Before beginning any curriculum unit, provide an introduction letter that covers (see Appendix C):
  - What the topic is.
  - Why it is being covered.
  - What the children will be learning.
  - How they will learn it.
  - Examples of *learning at home*.
  - Connections to any *community-related* events,
- **Provide**
  - Monthly activity idea calendars.
    - One calendar I liked to provide was one celebrating something for every day of the year, outside of the "normal" holidays and celebrations. For example, January 8th is National Bubble Bath Day (Clark, 2004). See an example of a month's calendar in Appendix C.
  - Themed take-home bags (see Appendix C).
    - For each theme unit, I created 5 identical bags that included activities that supported the ones completed at school. Families checked the bags out to use at home, then returned them when finished. The bags were restocked with the consumable items and made available for the next family.
  - Each bag contained an introductory letter that gave instructions for each of the following activities:
    - At least one children's book.
      - One game (bingo, lotto, board game, often teacher-created).
      - One manipulative activity (puzzle, counters, beads, play-dough).

- Dramatic play props and activity starters.
- One sensory activity.
- One science experiment.
- A recipe and instructions for a healthy snack related to them (ingredients measured, appropriately wrapped, and provided).
- Additional resources and materials the family could keep, continuing the learning process at home.

- **Document and Share**
  - For those activities completed at school, *communication is vital* to connect learning goals.
    - Photos, videos, and live classroom streaming programs reinforce the connection to learning.
      - At the end of each week, I posted a photo documentation display of what was learned and captioned each one to make connections to milestones and standards.
      - Documentation can also be uploaded to Facebook, webpages, blogs, and other technology programs.
    - Create charts that families can see for each center that describes what is going on in each. For example:

In the Block Center, Children Learn

- *Math skills – counting, shapes, sizes, ordering, measuring.*
- *Science skills – stacking, textures, catapulting, rolling, and other principles of physics.*
- *Social skills – getting along with others, sharing, trading, compromising, and teamwork.*
- *Language skills – "shop" talk, new vocabulary, signs, symbols, shapes.*
- *Safety skills – keeping blocks out of mouths, following safety rules, no throwing, hitting, etc.*
- *Art skills – designing, drawing, "reading" blueprints.*
- *Gross motor skills – building, coordination, imitating.*
- *Fine-motor skills – small block manipulation, coordination, balance.*
- *Self-concept skills – I can do it! I'm having fun, making choices, completing tasks, accomplishing tasks!*

Family engagement is most effective when it is firmly established in the home as an important aspect of the educational process (Goodall & Montgomery, 2014; Murray et al., 2015). Encouraging and supporting the family to invest in their child's educational experience strengthens academic and social development. Support in these areas is needed even more for children who may be considered at risk because of diversity indicators such as ethnic or economic backgrounds (Calzada et al., 2015; Mendez, 2010; Murray et al., 2015). When families connect what is learned at school and the ideas you provide to them, they understand the growth and development process. This, in turn, gives them the foundation to expand on these ideas to offer their own at-home learning activities.

Connecting Learning in the Community to Family Engagement

As outlined in Chapter 2, family engagement extends to the community. When looking at family engagement within the community, it is essential to look at the social contexts and interactions as identified by Bronfenbrenner (1974), such as the rules and regulations set by society (McNeal, 2015). Naturally, microsystem contexts such as peers and family also affect the family engagement dynamic (McNeal, 2015; Sánchez & Walsh, 2017). The microsystem is comprised of the home, program, and family. The mesosystem's context is the *interactions* between the child, family, program, and the community. These interactions are also affected by the significant contexts of cultural and societal beliefs, values, and practices. The community is tasked with providing support and resources for children and families, at a minimum, in the areas of health, wellness, and education. Ideally, the community members should ensure that early childhood programs are offered and support them through resources and opportunities. However, these resources are often lacking, and early childhood practitioners are tasked with forcing themselves into the community (Mendez, 2010; Sánchez & Walsh, 2017).

Practitioners must seek out relationships with community members to find the resources needed to support families. These resources include programs and agencies that support the family with health and wellness, financial stability, cultural equity, and parenting skills. When practitioners employ the use of these resources, both the child and family benefit in a variety of ways. The most important result is demonstrating respect for the families' strengths and efforts in their role as the child's primary caregiver and teacher (Erdener & Knoeppel, 2018; NAEYC, 2009, 2010). The family's cultural background and belief system are also supported and respected by the program, leading children to respect these as well (Epstein, 2001). Equally as necessary, the family is more inclined to place a high value on the importance of early education, thus supporting academic achievement and social-emotional development (Hilado, Kallemeyn, Leow, Lundy, & Israel, 2011). When family members feel supported in their role, they are more inclined to engage in a partnership with the program and practitioners (Epstein, 2001). Families also benefit from increased access to support services and connections with other families (Epstein, 2001).

Children benefit through access to extracurricular experiences that may not otherwise be afforded to them because of financial limitations or other constraints. As collaborative relationships expand, children become aware of the many career options available as well as future educational experiences. Children learn to be participative members of a community and how to access services for support (Epstein, 2001) Practitioners benefit by developing respect for family strengths and efforts in their role in the child's education and developing ongoing relationships with community services and agencies (Epstein, 2001; Hilado et al., 2011). Practitioners become more aware of available community resources and services to enhance curriculum and teaching practices and becoming more knowledgeable in assisting families with referrals to needed services (Epstein, 2001; Morrison et al., 2015). Practitioners also become more aware of available community resources and services to enhance curriculum and teaching practices and more knowledgeable in assisting families with referrals to needed services (Epstein, 2001; Morrison et al., 2015).

Community collaboration can be challenging in many ways, including finding the resources and services that meet the needs of the families (Epstein, 2001). One of the prime barriers to community support lies within the social status of the field. Early childhood education is still misunderstood and viewed as a baby-sitting service rather than education (Mahmood, 2013). Many community agencies may also be reluctant to enter collaborative relationships based on available funding and employee service hours (Hornby & Lafaele, 2011). Because of these and other factors, practitioners may have difficulty locating services to collaborate with to support families.

Strategies for Learning in the Community

How can this be achieved through your program policy? First, community relationships must be established. As outlined in the previous chapters, start with *sharing* your Vision and Mission statements and other information with community members. There are many ways to get connected with your community – some suggestions follow.

- **Inform**
    - Create a community packet that shares brief information about your program, including the Vision and Mission statements. Think of where you can place these – agencies and programs that support families.
    - Let them know in a brief letter how you can support them and vice versa.
    - Provide them with flyers to hand out to their clients/customers.
    - Ask to write a regular column in local newspapers or online blogs.
    - Share information about community events and encourage the families to attend and support.
- **Invite them!**
    - Ask community programs and agencies to come to your program and share what they can do for families.
    - Ask them to present programs for the children (dentist, doctor, library, and other "community helpers"). Invite the helpers to come to you. Field trips are great, but when they come to you, they learn about what you do. Often, your families are your first line of connection!
    - Invite your local and state lawmakers – they *need* to know what you do for the community.
- **Barter**
    - Offer community members free advertising in your materials in exchange for them advertising for you!
    - You can also exchange for monetary sponsorship, such as the take-home activity bags. "This take-home activity was sponsored by . . ." – quid pro quo (this for that).

- **Represent**
  - Set up booths at local health fairs or other community events. One extraordinarily successful event my program participated in was the Kentucky State Fair. Since Louisville is the Kentucky Derby's home, we gathered tons of newspapers and made free Derby hats for all passersby. Each hat's décor simply included our business card. That activity landed us on the evening news not once but three times throughout the fair's two-week run.
  - Host your own community event and invite external programs to represent! Want to host a family carnival? Invite the community to set up games or concessions!
- **Create Relationships**
  - Start communicating with businesses that you may not relate to children or families. Hosting a family event where you will be serving food? Ask your local grocer if they would be willing to donate one item for the meal.
  - Let businesses know how you can help them. Again, in exchange for sponsorship or donation, could you hold 5 spots at a reduced rate in your program for their employees?

Children benefit from these relationships and connections through continuous support and development of skills and knowledge in the home, program, and community settings (Epstein, 2001; Summer & Summer, 2014). Children's self-identity is developed within these components of the ecological systems through meaningful activities and opportunities. The family's benefits include learning to support and encourage their children's educational development and increase their own knowledge of best practices in the process. Practitioners develop better methods for planning individualized curriculum through the relationships formed with families and community members.

It is once again time to put your creative juices to work. For learning at home, think about the ideas shared here (please, feel free to USE them). For building our community learning relationships, think about what was learned on Sesame Street – who are the people in your neighborhood, and how can they help? Use the following illustration and the next worksheet to start outlining your policy on supporting learning at home and in the community.

Extending Learning in the Home and Community

Figure 7.1 The People in Your Neighborhood

Kathryn E. McKay

Worksheet 4. Learning in the Home and Community – Policy

Parent Handbook	Educator Handbook
WHY:	**WHY:**
WHO:	**WHO:**
WHAT:	**WHAT**
WHERE:	**WHERE:**
WHEN:	**WHEN:**
HOW:	**HOW:**

References

Bronfenbrenner, U. (1974). Developmental research, public policy, and the ecology of childhood. *Child development, 45*(1), 1–5.

Brown, J. R., Knoche, L. L., Edwards, C. P., & Sheridan, S. M. (2009). Professional development to support parent engagement: A case study of early childhood practitioners. *Early Education & Development, 20*, 482–506. https://doi.org/10.1080/10409280902783475

Calzada, E. J., Huang, K., Hernandez, M., Soriano, E., Acra, C. F., Dawson-McClure, S., Brotman, L. (2015). Family and teacher characteristics as predictors of parent involvement in education during early childhood among Afro-Caribbean and Latino immigrant families. *Urban Education, 50*, 870–896. https://doi.org/10.1177/0042085914534862

Clark, S. (2004). *Every day a holiday: Celebrations for the whole year.* Grand Rapids, MI: Revell.

Demircan, Ö., & Erden, F. T. (2015). Parental involvement and developmentally appropriate practices: A comparison of parent and teacher beliefs. *Early Child Development and Care, 185*, 209–225. https://doi.org/10.1080/03004430.2014.919493

Epstein, J. (2001). *School, family, and community partnerships: Preparing educators and improving schools.* Boulder, CO: Westview Press.

Erdener, M. A., & Knoeppel, R. C. (2018). Parents' perceptions of their involvement in schooling. *International Journal of Research in Education and Science, 4*, 1–13. https://doi.org/10.21890/ijres.369197

Goodall, J., & Montgomery, C. (2014). Parental involvement to parental engagement: A continuum. *Educational Review, 66*, 399–410. https://doi.org/10.1080.00131911.2013.781576

Grindal, T., Bowne, J. B., Yoshikawa, H., Schindler, H. S., Duncan, G. J., Magnuson, K., & Shonkoff, J. P. (2016). The added impact of parenting education in early childhood education: A meta-analysis. *Children and Youth Services Review, 70*, 238–249. https://doi.org/10.1016/j.childyouth.2016.09.018

Halgunseth, L. C., Petereson, A., Stark, D. R., & Moodie, S. (2009). *Family engagement, diverse families, and early childhood education programs: An integrated review of the literature.* Washington, DC: NAEYC.

Hilado, A. V., Kallemeyn, L., Leow, C., Lundy, M., & Israel, M. (2011). Supporting child welfare and parent involvement in preschool programs. *Early Childhood Education Journal, 39,* 343–353. https://doi.org/10.1007/s10643-011-0471-z

Hornby, G., & Lafaele, R. (2011). Barriers to parental involvement in education: An explanatory model. *Educational Review, 63,* 37–52. https://doi.org/10.1080/00131911.2018.1388612

Ihmeideh, F., & Oliemat, E. (2015). The effectiveness of family involvement in early childhood programmes: Perceptions of kindergarten principal and teachers. *Early Child Development and Care, 185,* 181–197. https://doi.org/10.1080/03004430.2014.915817

Kellar-Guenther, Y., Rosenberg, S. A., Block, S. R., & Robinson, C. C. (2014). Parent involvement in early intervention: What role does setting play? *Early Years: An International Journal of Research and Development, 34,* 81–93. https://doi.org/10.1080/09575146.2013.823382

Mahmood, S. (2013). First-year preschool and kindergarten teachers: Challenges of working with parents. *School Community Journal, 23*(2), 55–85. Retrieved from https://files.eric.ed.gov/fulltext/EJ1028824.pdf

Manz, P. H., Gernhart, A. L., Bracaliello, C. B., Pressimone, V. J., & Eisenberg, R. A. (2014). Preliminary development of the parent involvement in early learning scale for low-income families enrolled in a child-development-focused home visiting program. *Journal of Early Intervention, 36,* 171–191. https://doi.org/10.1177/1053815115573077

McNeal, R. B. (2015). Parent involvement and student performance: The influence of school context. *Educational Research for Policy and Practice, 14,* 153–167. https://doi.org/10.1007/s10671-014-9167-7

McWayne, C. M., Melzi, G., Schick, A. R., Kennedy, J. L., & Mundt, K. (2013). Defining family engagement among Latino Head Start parents: A mixed-methods measurement development study. *Early Childhood Research Quarterly, 28,* 593–607. https://doi.org/10.1016/j.ecresq.2013.03.008

Mendez, J. L. (2010). How can parents get involved in preschool? Barriers and engagement in education by ethnic minority parents of children attending Head Start. *Cultural Diversity and Ethnic Minority Psychology, 16,* 26–36. https://doi.org/10.1037/a0016258

Morrison, J. W., Storey, P., & Zhang, C. (2015). Accessible family involvement in early childhood programs. *Dimensions of Early Childhood,*

39(3), 33–38. Retrieved from www.southernearlychildhood.org/upload/pdf/Accessible_Family_Involvement_in_Early_Childhood_Programs_by_Johnetta_W__Morrison_Pamela_Storey_and_Chenyi_Zhang.pdf

Murray, E., McFarland-Piazza, L., & Harrison, L. J. (2015). Changing patterns of parent-teacher communication and parent involvement from preschool to school. *Early Child Development and Care, 185*, 1031–1052. https://doi.org/10.1080/03004430.2014.975223

National Association for the Education of Young Children. (2009). *Developmentally appropriate practice in early childhood programs serving children from birth through age 8*. Washington, DC: NAEYC.

National Association for the Education of Young Children. (2010). *Engaging diverse families project*. Retrieved from www.naeyc.org/familyengagement/about

Nitecki, E. (2015). Integrated school-family partnerships in preschool: Building quality involvement through multidimensional relationships. *School Community Journal, 25*, 195–219. Retrieved from https://files.eric.ed.gov/fulltext/EJ1085725.pdf

Sánchez, C., & Walsh, B. (2017). Meeting national expectations for partnering with families. *Dimensions of Early Childhood, 45*(2), 20–28. Retrieved from www.southernearlychildhood.org/page.php?purl=seca_publications

Schaub, M. (2015). Is there a home advantage in school readiness for young children? Trends in parent engagement in cognitive activities with young children, 1991–2001. *Journal of Early Childhood Research, 13*, 47–63. https://doi.org/10.1177/1476718X12468122

Share, M., & Kerrins, L. (2013). Supporting parental involvement in children's early learning: Lessons from community childcare centres in Dublin's Docklands. *Child Care in Practice, 19*, 355–374. https://doi.org/10.1080/13575279.2013.799457

Summer, M., & Summer, G. L. (2014). Creating family learning communities. *YC: Young Children, 69*(4), 8–14. Retrieved from www.jstor.org/stable/ycyoungchildren.69.4.8

Sy, S. R., Gottfried, A. W., & Gottfried, A. E. (2013). A transactional model of parental involvement and children's achievement from early childhood through adolescence. *Parenting: Science & Practice, 13*, 133–152. https://doi.org/10.1080/15295192.2012.709155

Weiss, H., Caspe, M., & Lopez, M. E. (2006). *Family involvement in early childhood education*. Cambridge, MA: Harvard University, Harvard Family Research Project.

Whyte, K. L., & Karabon, A. (2016). Transforming teacher – Family relationships: Shifting roles and perceptions of home visits through the Funds of Knowledge approach. *Early Years: Journal of International Research & Development, 36*(2), 207. https://doi.org/10.1080/09575146.2016.1139546

Decision Making and Goal Setting With Families

Thus far, you have been adding layers to your foundation of family engagement. The principles have intentionally been put in a specific order for building purposes. Each layer forms the foundation for the next. Now that you have understood and created how you will support families through relationships, communication, and learning activities, you can make the policy plan for including them in the process. It is not enough to have the activities discussed thus far. You must plan for how the family can make decisions and set goals mutually beneficial to the child, the family, and the practitioners. However, this process is a bit easier because of all the foundational legwork you have completed thus far.

In NAEYC's principle 1 (2010), practitioners are tasked with actively *welcoming and inviting* families to share in making decisions about their child's education. Through joint goal setting, the child's learning is reinforced at home, and families better understand the program's learning process. In Chapter 8, you will build the next layer of your policy to include the family in decision-making processes for the child's education.

The need for program practitioners to include families in decisions concerning their child's education has been a recurring theme in family engagement research. The first principle for family engagement is including families in the decision-making and goal-setting process for their child (NAEYC, 2010). This simply means that practitioners and family members come together to set goals for the child's learning both in the home (learning at home) and within the program. As indicated in previous chapters, practitioners should actively welcome and invite families to share in the process of decision making as it concerns their child's education. Through joint goal setting, the child's learning is reinforced at home, and families have a better understanding of the program's learning process (NAEYC, 2010).

Additionally, next to the family, practitioners are the primary adults in a child's life, indicating the need for a collaborative relationship within the decision-making process (Alacam & Olgan, 2017; Hilado, Kallemeyn, Leow, Lundy, & Israel, 2011). To create this type of relationship, practitioners need to be highly skilled in engaging family members. Yet, research indicated that preservice and entry-level practitioners have low to moderate skills in implementing any parent involvement strategies. Further, preservice courses offer little to no coverage of *how* to implement relationships with the families they will serve (Alacam & Olgan, 2017). The No Child Left Behind Act (NCLB) of 2008 directed educational programs to offer ample opportunities for participation in the decisions regarding the child's education (Morrison, Storey, & Zhang, 2015; Tran, 2014). Specifically, the NCLB addressed the concept that family members play an integral role in their child's learning. As such, practitioners should encourage the active involvement of the family in the program and support parents to be full partners in the decision-making process (Ma, Shen, Krenn, Hu, & Yuan, 2016; Tran, 2014). Including and supporting the family in the decision-making process allows them to have shared control. In turn, they influence their child's education. Their academic achievement levels are also higher, regardless of adverse issues such as poverty or cultural background.

Research also has indicated higher motivation for families to engage in their child's education when *explicitly invited* specifically by practitioners to share in making decisions (Baker, Wise, Kelley, & Skiba, 2016; Ihmeideh & Oliemat, 2015; Shen, Washington, Bierlein Palmer, & Xia, 2014). Practitioners must address any barriers that keep families from engaging and participating. Barriers significantly affect the ability of families to engage. For example, choosing times that work best for each family to meet for decision making and goal setting. Merely offering to work around the families' schedules increases the likelihood of participation (Baker et al., 2016).

Some research has also suggested *the child* be an integral member of the decision-making and goal-setting partnership (Ghiratto & Mazzoni, 2013; Nitecki, 2015). Children have the right to be a participant in all matters that affect them in harmony with the adults in their world. In doing so, the context of relationships is built on trust, kindness, and genuine care (Ghiratto & Mazzoni, 2013; Summer & Summer, 2014). The decisions and goals of the child, after all, are going to be completed by him or her. Practitioners allow children to pursue their own interests and make choices in the classroom. The child should also be allowed to plan the activities they participate in, like creating their own lesson plan. Of course, guidance from the adults in the partnership is crucial. Ultimately, the purpose of shared decision making is to identify educational goals and objectives for the child. While there is a shared interest in the child's success, the *expectations* of the child, the family, and the practitioners may differ. As noted by Bronfenbrenner, this is primarily based on each member's diverse backgrounds, beliefs, and values (Hornby & Lafaele, 2011).

There are some challenges to shared decision making and goal setting. Time, money, language barriers, and the program's ability to engage all families because of their diverse backgrounds are just a few examples (Epstein, 2001; Morrison et al., 2015). Other challenges include the fact that many program administrators and practitioners lack leadership skills themselves. In turn, it would be difficult for practitioners to lead family members in their own leadership roles, which are discussed in Chapter 9. In these cases, practitioners would need to seek outside training sources to develop these skills. Doing so will ultimately lead to increased costs associated with implementing family engagement policies and practices (Epstein, 2001).

There are many benefits, however, when shared decision making is implemented and supported in programs. Children benefit by observing the family's participation in their educational program, and it emphasizes the child as their priority (Epstein, 2001). Children also begin to understand the process of decision making when each member shares different opinions, ideas, and views to achieve shared goals in positive interactions (Epstein, 2001). Benefits for the family members include having their thoughts and beliefs heard and discussed, even if the results did not favor or include their views or ideas. They do, however, experience the feeling of ownership in their child's educational goals and objectives.

Additionally, families benefit by becoming more aware of the rules and regulations that govern the program, such as licensing requirements and state early learning standards (Epstein, 2001; Nitecki, 2015). Shared decision making also allows practitioners to better understand parent perspectives for foundational concepts in policy development and establishing partnerships with family members (Epstein, 2001; Nitecki, 2015). Shared decision making reinforces the concepts of two-way communication,

Family Decision-Making and Goal Setting

reciprocal relationships, and learning in the home and the community. Ultimately, when families (and the child) are involved, relationships based on respect rather than power and control are created (Epstein, 2001; Epstein & Sheldon, 2016; Halgunseth, Petereson, Stark, & Moodie, 2009; Nitecki, 2015; Weiss, Caspe, & Lopez, 2006).

Here and in the previous chapters, you have learned about the components of welcoming and inviting families to engage. Combined with what has been shared in this chapter, how might you create this portion of the policy to engage families in making decisions and setting goals? The good news is, you have already started. By building the previous layers of relationships, communication, and learning experiences, you have provided families with the information they need to make informed decisions. To connect this section of the policy, an example scenario that connects each of these components is outlined in the following paragraphs.

> You have enrolled 3-year-old Carsen and his family in your program. Through the **intake survey**, you have learned that both of his parents are middle-school teachers and that Carsen has an older sibling (10 year age difference). You have also acquired important contextual information such as where they live and their personal beliefs, values, and practices as parents. As part of the enrollment process, you have also asked the family to fill out a brief **developmental questionnaire** to get a feel for his current developmental status. You also have provided the family with the **communication survey** and have learned that dad will be the one who will drop off, and mom will pick up. Both have indicated they would like to have text messages for urgent issues but prefer to have other information in the form of discussions at drop off and pick up.
>
> In the parent questionnaire, it appears Carsen is on target for most developmental domains. He seems, though, to have issues within the social-emotional domain, specifically in playing with unfamiliar peers (developmental milestone). You share with the family that this is **where you would like to start creating goals** for Carsen and **provide them with a copy of the developmental milestones for three-year-old** children. Additionally, you **give them a copy of the early learning guidelines for your state** to review. You point out one that explicitly references the child's ability to play with others. You then **ask the family to provide contextual information** on how Carsen plays with others at home and other social gatherings outside the program.
>
> **Using this information, you create some goals and activities to support Carsen's learning in this area, then share them with the family for their input.**

Family Decision-Making and Goal Setting

Together, you modify the goals to best meet the child's needs in all surroundings (home, program, community). You have agreed to **send weekly reports to keep the family up to date** on Carsen's progress toward the goals. With each account, you will **share one activity the family can do together in the home** to support Carsen's work on this goal. The **family is asked to share the results of their participation in the activity in the provided** notebook. You are also aware (through communications) that the family is involved in their church. You have **suggested other faith-based activities in the community** that will allow Carsen to continue his goal development.

Three months after Carsen has been in your program, **you schedule a family conference to discuss this and other developmental goals that he has achieved**. In this meeting, everyone, **including Carsen**, has agreed that he has met the goal of playing with unfamiliar peers. **After reviewing his progress, the group identifies his next set of goals**.

In this scenario, all the foundational principles of family engagement are outlined in bold type. As the practitioner, you developed a relationship, provided two-way communication, and related activities for the home and the community. Thus, the policy you will create for this is totally up to you and based on your program. Of course, you also likely will address the prior components of the family engagement policy you have developed. There still will be a need to clearly communicate the process you will use for implementing each piece.

As with the policy's previous components, you will continue to address the "who, what, where, when, why, and how" questions. There will be overlapping of details, activities, and wording because each policy affects the others, as indicated in the scenario. When the policies begin to merge and overlap somewhat, the *comprehensive system* becomes solidified, which is the goal to meet principle 6 – and why we started with this topic in Chapter 2. Creating policies and procedures for any component in an early childhood program becomes much like a "connect-the-dot" activity.

As you create a policy for including the family in decision making and goal setting, review the steps and activities introduced thus far.

- Information through Vision and Mission statements.
- Information gathering through intake surveys.
- Relationship building.
- Communication strategies.
- Connection of learning between the home, program, and community.

Creating a policy to meet principle 1 is highly dependent on the previous foundational layers. Using this information and the worksheet template, what process (policy) will you put into place to work with families in decision making and goal setting?

Worksheet 5. Policy for Decision-Making and Goal Setting – Families

Parent Handbook	Educator Handbook
WHY:	WHY:
WHO:	WHO:
WHAT:	WHAT
WHERE:	WHERE:
WHEN:	WHEN:
HOW:	HOW:

References

Alacam, N., & Olgan, R. (2017). Pre-service early childhood teachers' self-efficacy/beliefs towards parent involvement. *Teaching Education, 28,* 421–434. https://doi.org/10.1080/10476210.2017.1324843

Baker, T. L., Wise, J., Kelley, G., & Skiba, R. J. (2016). Identifying barriers: Creating solutions to improve family engagement. *School Community*

Journal, 26, 161–184. Retrieved from https://files.eric.ed.gov/fulltext/EJ1124003.pdf

Epstein, J. L. (2001). *School, family, and community partnerships: Preparing educators and improving schools.* Boulder, CO: Westview Press.

Epstein, J. L., & Sheldon, S. B. (2016). Necessary but not sufficient: The role of policy for advancing programs of school, family, and community partnerships. *The Russell Sage Foundation Journal of the Social Sciences, 2*(5), 202–219. https://doi.org/10.7758/rsf.2016.2.5.10

Ghiratto, L., & Mazzoni, V. (2013). Being part, being involved: The adult's role and child participation in an early childhood learning context. *International Journal of Early Years Education, 21,* 300–308. https://doi.org/10.1080/09669760.2013.867166

Halgunseth, L. C., Peteroson, A., Stark, D. R., & Moodie, S. (2009). *Family engagement, diverse families, and early childhood education programs: An integrated review of the literature.* Washington, DC: NAEYC.

Hilado, A. V., Kallemeyn, L., Leow, C., Lundy, M., & Israel, M. (2011). Supporting child welfare and parent involvement in preschool programs. *Early Childhood Education Journal, 39,* 343–353. https://doi.org/10.1007/s10643-011-0471-z

Hornby, G., & Lafaele, R. (2011). Barriers to parental involvement in education: An explanatory model. *Educational Review, 63,* 37–52. https://doi.org/10.1080/00131911.2018.1388612

Ihmeideh, F., & Oliemat, E. (2015). The effectiveness of family involvement in early childhood programmes: Perceptions of kindergarten principal and teachers. *Early Child Development and Care, 185,* 181–197. https://doi.org/10.1080/03004430.2014.915817

Ma, X., Shen, J., Krenn, H. Y., Hu, S., & Yuan, J. (2016). A meta-analysis of the relationship between learning outcomes and parental involvement during early childhood education and early elementary education. *Education Psychology Review, 28,* 771–801. https://doi.org/10.1007/s10648-015-9351-1

Morrison, J. W., Storey, P., & Zhang, C. (2015). Accessible family involvement in early childhood programs. *Dimensions of Early Childhood, 39*(3), 33–38. Retrieved from www.southernearlychildhood.org/upload/pdf/Accessible_Family_Involvement_in_Early_Childhood_Programs_by_Johnetta_W__Morrison_Pamela_Storey_and_Chenyi_Zhang.pdf

National Association for the Education of Young Children. (2010). *Engaging diverse families project.* Retrieved from www.naeyc.org/familyengagement/about

Nitecki, E. (2015). Integrated school-family partnerships in preschool: Building quality involvement through multidimensional relationships. *School Community Journal, 25,* 195–219. Retrieved from https://files.eric.ed.gov/fulltext/EJ1085725.pdf

No Child Left Behind Act of 2001, 20 U.S.C. § 6319 (2008).

Shen, J., Washington, A. L., Bierlein Palmer, L., & Xia, J. (2014). Effects of traditional and nontraditional forms of parental involvement on school-level achievement outcome: An HLM study using SASS 2007–2008. *Journal of Educational Research, 107*(4), 326–337. https://doi.org/10.1080/00220671.2013.823368

Summer, M., & Summer, G. L. (2014). Creating family learning communities. *YC: Young Children, 69*(4), 8–14. Retrieved from www.jstor.org/stable/ycyoungchildren.69.4.8

Tran, Y. (2014). Addressing reciprocity between families and schools: Why these bridges are instrumental for students' academic success. *Improving Schools, 17,* 18–29. https://doi.org /10.1177/1365480213515296

Weiss, H., Caspe, M., & Lopez, M. E. (2006). *Family involvement in early childhood education.* Cambridge, MA: Harvard University, Harvard Family Research Project.

Decision Making and Goal Setting in the Program

Before we dig into the last principle for your family engagement policy, look at where you are now – almost to the end! You are probably saying "NO MORE!" at this point. However, there is still one aspect of engagement to cover. Think about your current work in your program – not enough hours in the day to get it all done, right? You would love to find the time to engage all families using what you have learned thus far. You would also love to get more involved in participating in advocacy events within the community. How might the development of this piece of family engagement policy support that burden? Family engagement principle 5 (NAEYC, 2010) encourages you to include families to assist with program-level decisions, goals, and advocacy efforts.

As identified in the previous chapter, it is essential to include the family in decision making and goal setting to support their children's education. They must also be included in the program decisions and goals that directly affect their roles and responsibilities as clients. For example, it is imperative to include their thoughts, ideas, and input in creating your family engagement policy. They are who you serve, and the policy really is all about them. Yes, you are including a policy that guides what the program provides for families. Still, the policy's primary purpose is to engage the family in the child's education and support the program's efforts in providing that education.

Why is this piece crucial to family engagement? The No Child Left Behind (NCLB) and Family Engagement Act of 2011 (U.S. Department of Health and Human Services: Department of Education, 2016) described engagement as the *shared responsibility* between the family and education program for supporting family and child success (Hilado, Kallemeyn, & Phillips, 2013; Morrison, Storey, & Zhang, 2015). You have learned that high-quality family engagement occurs when practitioners validate their participation as decision makers in their child's education. Families then become stakeholders of the program and are afforded the right to assist in making program decisions (Hilado et al., 2013).

Supporting families to advocate for themselves is equally important. Not only is the family considered to be the child's first teacher, but they also are the child's primary advocate (Brown, Knoche, Edwards, & Sheridan, 2009; Halgunseth, Petereson, Stark, & Moodie, 2009). Some families may even participate in advocacy groups to lobby for better child development policies (Hilado et al., 2013). Regardless of how they become involved, networking begins, building stronger relationships. Through both program-level decision making and participation as advocates, family engagement is encouraged and supported for their child's growth, development, and education from birth through adulthood (Erdener & Knoeppel, 2018).

Decision Making and Goal Setting for the Program

In program-level engagement, the family members are again invited to participate by making decisions and creating goals for the entire program. Subsequently, engagement at this level also includes guiding family members into leadership and representative roles within the program and possibly within the community (Epstein, 2001). Families who are supported through various methods, such as in the prior levels of engagement, will feel more comfortable being engaged at the program level. Program-level engagement encompasses all other levels, as you will see later. What might this policy include for your program?

- Use family surveys, suggestion boxes, and face-to-face conversations to really "hear" what they are saying to you.
  - Ask them what they need to feel fully supported.
- Provide information and data on licensing regulation requirements, NAEYC's Developmentally Appropriate Practice (DAP), and the Code of Ethical Conduct (NAEYC, 2011) to inform the decision-making

process. The more they know, the more they will understand and support all policies.
- Create committees, forums, and/or focus groups for each area of policy that involves them, such as:
  - Communication strategies.
  - Events.
  - Holidays (why they are included or excluded, for example).
  - Emergency preparedness.
  - Health, safety, and nutrition.
  - Schedules and curriculum.
  - Alternate care and substitutes.
  - Guidance strategies.
  - Field trips.
  - Transportation.
- Create a family mentoring program where the longer-term families can mentor and support engaging new families.

Again, when families are involved in program decisions and goals, policies' implementation will likely be more successful. Managing some of the overall goals of the program can be shared with those who are affected most – the families. Children receive consistent messages about their program and education. Most important, however, is the more in-depth understanding and connection (relationships) between practitioners and families. NAEYC's updated DAP (2020) statement shares that practitioners should identify commonality, individuality, and context for supporting decision making in children's learning. The same can be said for working with families. Addressing the commonalities between the program and the families served, respecting and supporting families' unique qualities, and knowing, respecting, and supporting their contexts will lead to better decisions and goals for all involved.

As engagement practices grow and develop, families should be encouraged to participate further in such activities as becoming a member of a Parent Advisory Council (PAC). They may also become a representative for all families on the board of directors or serve on family-oriented committees both in and outside the program (Epstein, 2001; NAEYC, 2010). If you have included families in the engagement policy's previous steps, you have provided them with the information and tools they need to become leaders in the program.

Engaging Families as Advocates

The second aspect of this level of engagement involves teaching families to advocate first for themselves and their children, then for those who govern the field of early childhood education. The field is certainly front and center in the news. It is no secret that the U.S. is falling short in many areas. While great strides have been made, there is still much ground to cover to provide a *high-quality and equitable* education for our youngest citizens. Once families have a solid understanding of your program, they can then be given information about local, state, and even national issues that directly affect them. It is the practitioner's role to provide information to families and give them the tools needed to become advocates. Once families become fully engaged, they may desire to become involved in advocacy to support the program's needs and improvement of the field. Practitioners are often involved in advocating for family services that are fair and responsive to family needs. They should also provide family members with the resources and materials to help them become advocates (Epstein, 2001; NAEYC, 2010; Sánchez & Walsh, 2017).

Advocacy Tools for Practitioners and Families

Early childhood advocacy builds support for issues concerning the well-being and needs of young children and their families among the public, elected officials, the media, and key opinion leaders. Activities can include:

- Educating audiences about a topic.
- Sharing illustrative stories.
- Working on a solution to a problem.

Individual citizens can always contact elected officials as constituents and are not regulated by state or federal governments. However, it is essential to use personal e-mail and telephone information when contacting policy-makers. Activities that practitioners can participate in include:

- Inviting legislators to visit your program and hear about the work you do.
- Providing policymakers with information and educational materials on child growth and development topics. This should be research-based

and not self-serving. Ideally, policymakers want to know how it affects their constituents, not those who "profit."
- Sharing through media about a specific social issue – sticking to the facts and only how it affects young children.
- Actively tracking bills, legislative positions, and voting records of political candidates. NAEYC has a page on their website where you can find information about your state.

Everyone involved in advocacy efforts must understand that the goal is to improve the lives of children and families. This is done by providing information to influence policymakers' opinions and activities. As part of their responsibilities, public officials are required to solicit advice from the people they represent. Who better than those involved in and served by the field to provide that information? Practitioners and family members must be equipped with the knowledge needed to accurately engage in these activities.

According to The Ounce of Prevention Fund's Early Childhood Advocacy Kit (2009), there are different advocacy types. These are outlined briefly in the following list.

- Case advocacy – intervening to address an individual child or family's problem.
    - Strategies include researching rules or eligibility requirements of a particular program or policy.
    - Document the situation, its history, and whether others have had similar difficulties.
    - File an appeal if services are denied or changes not implemented.
- Administrative advocacy – addressing the creation or revision of policies and resolving problems through activities that specifically target administrative and governmental agencies with the authority and discretion to change rules and regulations.
    - Strategies include:
        - Forming relationships with members of a specific agency to influence their decision making.
        - Participation in committees where decisions are made.
        - The sharing of research-based information about the impact of policy decisions in your community or other programs.

- Legislative advocacy – working with elected officials to educate them about policies or programs and inform them of the program's impact in their home district.
    - Strategies include:
        - Sending communications to policymakers via letters, e-mails, phone calls, or conducting personal visits.
        - Testifying about specific issues before legislative committees.
        - Working with local and state legislators to persuade parties to consider your proposal.
        - Meeting with representatives of the governor's office and local/state officials to gain attention for your issue.
        - Inviting legislators to visit your program for firsthand knowledge of how policies affect people in your program and community.
- Media advocacy – using media to increase public awareness and influence broader public debate about early childhood issues.
    - Strategies include:
        - Expressing your point of view through letters to the editor and call-in opportunities.
        - Contacting local reporters when your organization has news to share.
        - Researching how you might be a guest on local talk shows or public-affairs programs to share your expertise.
        - Meeting with the editors of local newspapers.
        - Identifying families or other impacted organizations and asking them to write letters or make calls as well.
        - Sharing pertinent information with elected officials from your community.

Early childhood organizations such as NAEYC are excellent resources to build an advocacy toolkit for family, program, and community use. Community members are, after all, stakeholders in early childhood programs. Without programs for children, their employees would not be able to work – early childhood is an essential piece of Bronfenbrenner's systems. Working together, families and practitioners can create and support awareness of the importance of early childhood education and build support for improving local, state, and federal policies for all.

When families are involved in a program's decision-making process, their rights to be heard and supported are valued. They also benefit by having the ability to input thoughts and ideas into policies and procedures that affect their children. There is a deepening of networking with other families and a feeling of ownership in their child's education. Engaging families at this level helps them develop leadership and representative (advocacy) roles within the program and the community. It gives family members a voice in the program's governance. Just as we afford families respect as their child's first teacher, we must afford respect in obtaining their input on matters that pertain to them. Throughout this book, you have been guided toward including the family in this policy-creation process. Again, no one knows each family's particular needs or wants but them! The very foundation of NAEYC's Developmentally Appropriate Practice (2009) is to provide fair and responsive services to family needs. Thus, the need to include family members in decision making and goal setting at the program level is essential. Ask them what they need!

At this point, you have supported stronger families through a solid family engagement plan. You have provided what they need to know and understand regarding early childhood programs' inner workings. Engagement at this level does not give carte-blanche freedom to create rules and regulations. It provides an opportunity for buy-in and support for the program's overall goals – think about your Vision and Mission. Everything must tie back to the program's Vision and Mission statement. It can be as involved as creating a parent advisory board or as simple as using some of the aforementioned surveys to gather input from families toward program improvement.

Your final piece of the policy puzzle requires you to identify once again what you will provide for families and what they can expect from you. Will you create a parent advisory council if you do not have one or make improvements if you do? How will practitioners engage families in the overall decision-making and goal-setting process regarding policies and procedures? What advocacy activities will you participate in, and how will families be involved?

For the last piece of your family engagement policy, once again, use the following worksheet to start outlining this aspect of your engagement policy. At this point, you may want to peek at the outlines in Appendices D and E to help you solidify your last piece of family engagement policy.

Worksheet 6 Policy Decision Making and Goal Setting – Prog. and Advocacy

Parent Handbook	Educator Handbook
WHY:	WHY:
WHO:	WHO:
WHAT:	WHAT
WHERE:	WHERE:
WHEN:	WHEN:
HOW:	HOW:

References

Brown, J. R., Knoche, L. L., Edwards, C. P., & Sheridan, S. M. (2009). Professional development to support parent engagement: A case study of early childhood practitioners. *Early Education & Development, 20*, 482–506. https://doi.org/10.1080/10409280902783475

Epstein, J. (2001). *School, family, and community partnerships: Preparing educators and improving schools.* Boulder, CO: Westview Press.

Erdener, M. A., & Knoeppel, R. C. (2018). Parents' perceptions of their involvement in schooling. *International Journal of Research in Education and Science, 4*, 1–13. https://doi.org/10.21890/ijres.369197

Halgunseth, L. C., Petereson, A., Stark, D. R., & Moodie, S. (2009). *Family engagement, diverse families, and early childhood education programs: An integrated review of the literature*. Washington, DC: NAEYC.

Hilado, A. V., Kallemeyn, L., & Phillips, L. (2013). Examining understandings of parent involvement in early childhood programs. *Early Childhood Research & Practice, 15*(2).

Morrison, J. W., Storey, P., & Zhang, C. (2015). Accessible family involvement in early childhood programs. *Dimensions of Early Childhood, 39*(3), 33–38. Retrieved from www.southernearlychildhood.org/upload/pdf/Accessible_Family_Involvement_in_Early_Childhood_Programs_by_Johnetta_W__Morrison_Pamela_Storey_and_Chenyi_Zhang.pdf

National Association for the Education of Young Children. (2009; 2020). *Developmentally appropriate practice in early childhood programs serving children from birth through age 8*. Washington, DC: NAEYC.

National Association for the Education of Young Children. (2010). *Engaging diverse families project*. Retrieved from www.naeyc.org/familyengagement/about

National Association for the Education of Young Children. (2011). *Code of ethical conduct and statement of commitment*. Retrieved from www.naeyc.org

No Child Left Behind Act of 2001, 20 U.S.C. § 6319 (2008).

The Ounce of Prevention Fund. (2009). *Early childhood advocacy kit*. Retrieved from https://startearly.org/app/uploads/pdf/EarlyChildhoodAdvocacyToolkit.pdf

Sánchez, C., & Walsh, B. (2017). Meeting national expectations for partnering with families. *Dimensions of Early Childhood, 45*(2), 20–28. Retrieved from www.southernearlychildhood.org/page.php?purl=seca_publications

U.S. Department of Health and Human Services: Department of Education. (2016). *Policy statement on family engagement: From the early years to the early grades*. Retrieved from https://www2.ed.gov/about/inits/ed/earlylearning/files/policy-statement-on-family-engagement.pdf

Introducing and Implementing New Policies

You have made it to the finish line! You have created an outline to guide creating a policy that fully includes families and meets the principles for effective engagement. Hooray! Now what? Your head is probably swimming with new ideas and approaches that you want to implement. In the Appendices, I have included examples and blank forms for you to use. For each policy, family, and practitioner, there is an outline to guide your writing for placement in your handbooks.

It is crucial, however, to proceed carefully and cautiously. I recommend taking each policy one step at a time. For each step in the process, set a timeline and create the goals and objectives. You have started this by completing the activities in this book! Referring to Chapter 4, begin with the end in mind. When do you want to have the complete family engagement policy completed – within a year? If so, divide each principle into smaller time frames, such as two months. Some policies will be easier to create than others – adjust your time accordingly. As you have practiced throughout, use the following prompts as you plan.

- Define why the policy is essential to your program's goals.
- Consider who will serve on the committee for creating the policies. Will the members change with the different topics?
- What needs to be included for each piece that relates to your program and your families?
- Designate the roles and responsibilities for each member.
- Where, when, and how often will you need to meet?
- As a group, decide how the policy will be implemented.

Remember, it is crucial to include family members in this process of program-level decision making. It is also essential to review and revise as needed to ensure each policy fits your program's Vision and Mission, family needs and wants, and overall goals.

Begin with the Vision and Mission statement – create a committee with family members, practitioners, and community members to clearly identify each policy's goals. Once these have been established as "final," send a letter to your clientele indicating that you have begun the process of refreshing your policies to be more family-oriented. In this communication, you can invite family members to volunteer to participate in the various groups that will further establish these policies. Provide the committee topics (the principles) and let them select when and how they can participate. I suggest creating policies in the same order in which they have been presented here, as each one builds upon the previous. Implement one before moving on to the next. Evaluate each policy piece every so often to see if changes need to be made. It is a process that should be considered carefully and thoughtfully.

Keep in mind that Head Start has been doing family engagement for decades! Review their policy, as well as policies from states that have implemented policy. Some states to review include Arizona, Colorado, Illinois, and Maryland. Research information from the references I have included in this book, review the NAEYC website articles on family engagement, and review the information on the principles. Another great resource to have in your toolkit is the book *Families & Educators Together: Building Great Relationships that Support Young Children*. This book provides a deeper look at each of the family engagement principles and shares examples of what other programs are doing to engage in family relationships.

There are many positive outcomes from creating a policy to provide effective family engagement in your program. Head Start identified 7 outcomes that promote positive family and child outcomes (U.S. Department of Health and Human Services, Administration for Children and Families, Office of Head Start, National Center on Parent, Family, and Community Engagement, 2018).

- When practitioners and families collaborate, family well-being is supported.
- Families who are supported enhance their relationships with their children.

- The family engages in lifelong education of their child.
- Families become lifelong learners.
- Families are better able to help children transition from one learning environment to another.
- Families form connections to other families and community members.
- Families become advocates and leaders in the community and in the field.

Some other resources you might want to look into include:

- *Building Strong Foundations: Advancing Comprehensive Policies for Infants, Toddlers, and Families.* ZERO TO THREE: www.zerotothree.org/resources/series/building-strong-foundations-advancing-comprehensive-policies-for-infants-toddlers-and-families.
- Maryland Family Engagement Toolkit: https://marylandfamiliesengage.org/family-engagement-toolkit/.
- Family and Community Engagement, U.S. Department of Education www.ed.gov/parent-and-family-engagement.
- Family Engagement Toolkit – Build Initiative www.buildinitiative.org/FamilyEngagementToolkit.
- *The Art of Leadership: Engaging Families in Early Childhood Organizations* Exchange Press, 2016.
- *Family Engagement in Early Childhood Settings* Redleaf Press, 2018.

Finally, *enjoy the process* – the end product will reflect you and your program as it evolves and changes. Let me know how it goes – you can contact me at dr.t@handsonlearningece.com. I'm happy to assist you in this process!

Reference

U.S. Department of Health and Human Services, Administration for Children and Families, Office of Head Start, National Center on Parent, Family, and Community Engagement. (2018). *Head start parent, family, and community engagement framework.* Retrieved from https://eclkc.ohs.acf.hhs.gov/sites/default/files/pdf/pfce-framework.pdf

Appendix A
Family Communication Preferences

Let's keep in Touch! (write in or circle answers)	
Child's name:	
Parent/guardian name(s):	
Home phone:	
Work phone:	
Cell phone:	
Email address:	
Language at home: Would you like communication to be given in your home language? YES NO	
Preferred form of contact:	Phone Email In person Text message
Are you able to receive images via your cell phone?	Yes/No
Best time of day to reach you?	Morning Afternoon Evening
What forms of communication work best for you? For example, for our newsletter, would you prefer paper, text, email?	

Tracking Family Communications

Child/family name:
Contact information:
Methods preferred:

Date	Method	With	Reason	Notes	Follow-up Required?
	☐ Phone ☐ Email ☐ In person ☐ Note ☐ Other:	☐ Mom ☐ Dad ☐ Guardian ☐ Other:	☐ Positive feedback ☐ Developmental progress ☐ Behavior issue ☐ Other:		☐ Yes ☐ No
	☐ Phone ☐ Email ☐ In person ☐ Note ☐ Other:	☐ Mom ☐ Dad ☐ Guardian ☐ :	☐ Positive feedback ☐ Developmental progress ☐ Behavior issue ☐ Other:		☐ Yes ☐ No
	☐ Phone ☐ Email ☐ In person ☐ Note ☐ Other:	☐ Mom ☐ Dad ☐ Guardian ☐ Other:	☐ Positive feedback ☐ Developmental progress ☐ Behavior issue ☐ Other:		☐ Yes ☐ No
	☐ Phone ☐ Email ☐ In person ☐ Note ☐ Other:	☐ Mom ☐ Dad ☐ Guardian ☐ Other:	☐ Positive feedback ☐ Developmental progress ☐ Behavior issue ☐ Other:		☐ Yes ☐ No
	☐ Phone ☐ Email ☐ In person ☐ Note ☐ Other:	☐ Mom ☐ Dad ☐ Guardian ☐ Other:	☐ Positive feedback ☐ Developmental progress ☐ Behavior issue ☐ Other:		☐ Yes ☐ No

Appendix B
Family Intake Survey

1. Tell me about your family – who lives in the home?
2. What is the language spoken most at home?
3. What are your most precious family traditions?
4. What are your family's practices around food or mealtimes?
5. Do you usually eat family meals or eat on the run?
6. Do you have any special dietary preferences or needs?
7. What are your children's favorite foods?
8. Tell me about your hopes for your child.
9. Tell me your expectations for your child.
10. Tell me about any fears you have for your child.
11. Do you have any nondevelopmental concerns about or for your child?
12. What would you like to see in your child's program?
13. Do you have any concerns or questions about your child's development?
14. Does your child have any identified special needs?
15. Has your child traveled to locations outside our community? With family or to see family? Identify locations and length of time away.
16. Tell me about your child's typical day at home.

17. What is your child's morning routine, schedule, evening routine, and bedtime?
18. What is your child's favorite activity to play alone?
19. What is your child's favorite activity to play with others (siblings, peers, neighbors, adults)?
20. Does your child have any specific fears?
21. Did your child attend another program previously?
22. Tell me about your child's typical day at that program.
23. How do you prefer to receive information about your child's activities and experiences in our program?
24. What do you want to know most about your child's day?
25. Our program values your involvement. How would you like to be involved or engaged in our program?
26. Do you have any concerns or limitations regarding family engagement, such as work commitments or transportation needs?
27. What are some skills, interests, talents, or hobbies that you might share with our program?
28. What are your feelings and preferences surrounding holidays, special dates, and birthdays?
29. Are there any special holidays that your family celebrates or does not celebrate?
30. Do you have any concerns about celebrations in general?
31. What special family activities or events do you do throughout the year (weekly, monthly, annually, around holidays, and so on)?
32. Parenting is a tough job. What additional information or support might you need or want to support you in this job?

Reprinted with Permission by Mary Muhs M. Ed, 2019

Appendix B

 Family Engagement Survey

Supporting our families is very important to us, and we want to hear your voice! Please share below how you feel about your current level of engagement and support from the program using the scale provided.

    5 = Strongly Agree, 4 = Agree, 3 = Neutral, 2 = Disagree, 1 = Strongly Disagree, or N/A

    _____ I receive information on what I can do at home to help my child improve or advance his/her learning.

    _____I receive information on child development and other important aspects of my child's education.

    _____Practitioners meet with me face to face a minimum of one time each year to discuss my child's progress.

    _____Communications provided from the program meet my individual needs (written, phone calls, emails, texts, etc.).

    _____If I have questions, concerns, or comments about issues concerning my child, they are addressed in a timely manner.

    _____I am invited to engage in all aspects of the program.

    _____I am kept apprised of what is going on within the program.

    _____There are many different ways that I can engage with the program.

    _____The program provides opportunities for me to learn about important topics related to child development, parenting, and engaging.

    _____The program provides regular updates on my child's progress.

    _____The program provides information on developmental milestones.

    _____My child's individual learning needs are addressed in the classroom and activities.

    _____The program asks about our goals and hopes for our child's development.

    _____The program supports our cultural values and beliefs.

    _____The program invites me to participate in decision making for planning and policy.

    _____I am invited to engage in activities within the program.

    _____I am provided information about community services and educational opportunities.

    _____Family engagement is valued by the program.

    _____The program is friendly and welcoming to families and children.

Appendix C
Family Letter Introducing a Theme Unit

Hello Families!

It is that time of year when we will be celebrating and learning more about the Kentucky Derby! This unit will last about 3 weeks, and the children have already completed their Know/Want-to-Know chart to expand on their learning from last year. They are very excited to get started!

We will review the concepts of:

- The history of the Derby, including when it started, and why it is a tradition here in our area.
- How fireworks are made and how they work.
- What a steamboat is and how it works.
- How hot air balloons work.

In our learning areas, we will complete these activities (and many more):

- Science – we will explore steamboats and paddlewheels and create our own boats.
- Dramatic Play – we will alternate our themes to include a hot air balloon ride, a Pegasus parade, and, of course our own Derby.
- Math – we will learn about measuring with "hands."
- Language/Literacy – children will create their own invitations for our Derby Family Day.
- Music – we will learn about the bugle and how it is played, and learn "Run for the Roses" by Dan Fogelberg.

Appendix C

At Home:
We will once again have our Derby-themed take-home bags available for checkout. As you attend the Derby Festival events, we encourage you to also do the following:

- Create a family Derby-themed poster.
- Make paper roses to create the Garland of Roses and lilies for the Oaks garland.
- Measure items around your house using hands from each family member and discuss why/how these measurements are different.
- Create your own Derby treats, such as a Derby pie!
- Take a trip to Churchill Downs pre-Derby and tour the museum.

Happy Derby!

Derby Theme Activity Bag for Families

Dear Families,
As you are aware, we are working on our Kentucky Derby theme, and it is time to share our activities with you! In this bag, you will find the following activities (remember all materials are provided for you):

- Kentucky Derby winners lotto game.
- Two books to share with your child at home about horses and the Derby (ach book has discussion questions to share about what you've read).
- Math/manipulative activities including a hot air balloon number match file folder activity and horse puzzles (with patterns to create your own).
- Directions and materials to make your own horse puppets and suggested activities for use.
- Sensory activities – steamboat racing and horse washing.
- One science experiment – growing bluegrass, oats, and hay.
- One healthy snack recipe – oatmeal/apple muffins.

Appendix C

 Kentucky Derby Winners – Lotto Game

The materials provided for this game include the lotto cards (with H-O-R-S-E at the top), lotto tokens, and the "calling" cards with pictures. The objective of the game is to get a 5-in-a-row match, just as in bingo. There is a FREE space in the middle of each card. Everyone can take turns being the caller – the children can simply hold up the pictures, while older family members can name each horse as drawn. For example, the caller draws "H – Affirmed" – the card has the horse's name and the picture on it. Players look for the picture but also will learn the names and name recognition.

 Book One – *D Is for Derby: A Kentucky Derby Alphabet*

This book is beautifully illustrated and provides many of the important pieces of the Kentucky Derby's history, as well as how it is celebrated today. The book is written in poetry style and talks about jockeys, famous horses, Bluegrass farms, and a look at the big race! On each page, along with the storyline, information is provided for a deeper look. We suggest that the family read the book first to become familiar with some of the information before reading to the child. Inside the book, we have placed a few open-ended questions for discussion as you read the book together.

 Book Two – *Horses*

Horses do much more than race! This book with real-life photographs talks about the many different ways horses can be enjoyed. There are work horses, show horses, and horses just for riding, and different breeds are also discussed. As with book one, there are open-ended questions provided to spark discussion with your child.

Appendix C

Math Activity One – Horse Puzzles

There are three different horse puzzles provided in an envelope for you and your child to enjoy together. The puzzles range in difficulty from basic 4–5 piece puzzles of a horse to one you can put together piece by piece – or perhaps leg by leg! On the latter puzzle, children will learn the different parts of the horse such as hooves, mane, tail, and legs. Not only do the puzzles help with one-to-one correspondence, but there is also a little anatomy thrown in as well! Included in the envelope is a set for the child to keep for continued learning.

Math Activity Two – Hot Air Balloon Race Numbers

As you've seen in our prior take-home bags, we love file-folder activities, and this one is a favorite with the children at school. The file folder has two sides. On the inside, you find the colorful balloons floating in the air high above the Ohio River and the Bluegrass Horse Farms. Each balloon has a number, and the corresponding number of dots are on the baskets (gondolas). Children will first match the number with the dots, then, on the reverse side of the baskets, they can match number for number.

On the other side of the file folder there is a balloon racing game. Everyone gets their own balloon (provided) and the race advances by rolling the die. As the die is rolled, the child should say how many dots are showing, then count those spaces. The first one to the end wins!

Dramatic Play Puppets – Horses

In your take-home bag, you will find a large Ziplock bag with different colored socks, yarn, felt, and other materials to create your own horses! Instructions for making sock puppets are included, but it is best to let the children be as openly creative as they want to be. Each family member can make a horse puppet (Sire and Mare – dad/mom, colts or foals for the children). Also provided is a small pack of construction paper and crayons for the children to create backdrops for their horse puppets.

Appendix C

There are some "story starters" to inspire the children to act with their horse for a play or to race! The possibilities are endless – and, of course, the puppets are theirs to keep.

Sensory Activity One – Steamboat Race

The children love doing this activity at school, so we know they will love sharing it with you! We have studied about what makes boats float, move, and even about paddlewheels. For this activity, you will find a small blow-up pool and some plastic boats. Blow up the pool, fill it with water, and race the boats. You can experiment with water levels and other things that might move the boats faster.

Sensory Activity Two – Washing Horses

Along with the pool and boats, you will find some plastic horses, soap, and brushes. The children have learned about the care of horses on the farms, including washing them. Have some great fun washing your horses!

Growing Grass, Oats, and Hay – Science Experiment

In our classroom, the children know that their science activities are almost always based on the scientific process. We have a char in the science area that displays the steps in picture format:

- 🔍 Make observation
- ❓ Gather information and ask questions
- 💡 Develop a hypothesis (prediction)
- 🧪 Test the hypothesis (do the experiment)
- 📊 Record the results (charts, drawings, etc.)
- 📣 Share the results (discuss what happened with others)

127

Appendix C

In this science experiment, the children will use the scientific process to plant, grow, and observe the growing of three very important plants for horses – grass, oats, and hay! We have introduced the children to these for understanding that "bluegrass" is what the horses have in the fields where they run, and oats and hay produce food and bedding for them. Assist your child in finding information about how to grow each of these. We have provided soil, containers, seeds, and a journal to record their observations, predictions, and results for growing. Some questions they might ask include, "Is the bluegrass really blue?" Concepts to discuss might be how each plant grows, what it needs to grow, how fast it grows, and much more. Encourage your child to share their results with the class.

Healthy Snack Recipe – Easy Oatmeal/Apple Muffins

During our study, the children have learned that apples and oats are great snacks for horses. They are good for us, too! In the bag, the final items you will see are the following ingredients:

1 cup flour, all-purpose
1 cup oats, dry
1 1/2 teaspoon baking powder
1 teaspoon cinnamon
1/8 teaspoon salt
1 large egg
1 cup Greek yogurt, plain
1/2 cup applesauce, unsweetened
1/4 cup brown sugar
1 teaspoon vanilla extract
1 medium apple

To make this easy and healthy snack:
Preheat oven to 350°F. Spray a muffin tin with cooking spray and set aside.
In a large bowl, mix together flour, oats, baking powder, cinnamon, and salt. In a separate bowl, whisk together egg, yogurt, applesauce, brown sugar, and vanilla.

Gradually add dry ingredients to the wet and mix until just blended.

Peel and dice apple; fold into batter.

Pour evenly into muffin cups and bake for 20–22 minutes until a toothpick inserted into the center of a muffin comes out clean.

Allow to cool before serving.

We hope you enjoy these activities with your child, and maybe you will create a few extensions of your own! Please share in the notebook provided how your family used the materials and activities to learn more about horses, the Derby, and any extra activities you did with the materials! We love pictures, so if you want, please share some of those as well.

Happy Learning!

Your Child's Teachers

Appendix C

 # Great News – Positive Notes to Families

Great News!!!!!!

Today, while Bentley was working in the block area, I noticed that she was really intentional with building a barn for the horses we've added to the area. When other children asked what she was doing, she told them, "I'm building a safe barn for the horses and I'm going to feed them hay." A few children wanted to join her, and she gave them each a job to do. She demonstrated leadership and worked with the other children to create a really nice barn. She also demonstrated her ability to work cooperatively with others. She asked really great questions about what barns should include, and asked if she could look for barn pictures, which we helped her do. I've included a couple of photos I took while they were working – she wanted to make sure you could see what they all accomplished together. Bentley stated this was one of her favorite activities today!

(pictures here)

Example Newsletter

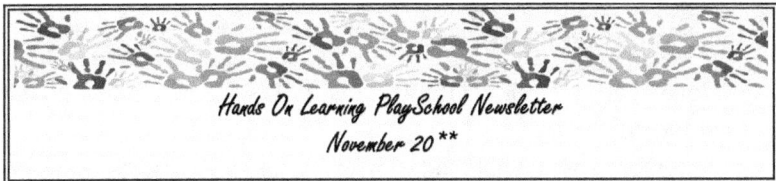

Hands On Learning PlaySchool Newsletter
*November 20**

November is a Time for Family!
Memories and Traditions
What traditions can you share with us?

Personal collection (McKay, 2021)

As a young child, some of my fondest memories are family gatherings for Thanksgiving. Dinner was always at my grandmother's house, and the whole family gathered – my parents, my aunt and uncle, and the cousins. I remember the sights, sounds, smells, and, of course, the taste of the delicious food! In our family there was no "kids table" – we all sat at the big dining room table with our family, and we used the "fine" china. Dinner was always turkey and stuffing, with green beans, cranberry salad, mashed potatoes, sweet potatoes, and my granny's super awesome homemade yeast rolls.

My grandparents lived on a farm, so it really was an "over-the-river-and-through-the-woods" experience. After the meal, the adults played card games, and the cousins and I would go outside to play – regardless of the weather. At that time in the 60s and 70s we played pilgrims and Indians. Later, when we were exhausted and cold, we would come in for desserts and hot apple cider. We usually ended up watching home movies. Those were our family traditions.

What traditions do you have for your family this month? Some may choose not to celebrate Thanksgiving, and that is okay – what traditions could you create with your family to celebrate YOU? Regardless of family structure, size, culture, background, values, or beliefs, it is important to celebrate who you are together – whatever that my look like!

From our family to yours – Happy November!

Upcoming Events!

Mark Your Calendars

November 1 – National Family Literacy Day – send your child with their favorite book!

November 3 – National Sandwich Day – make your favorite sandwich – send us the recipe and we will make for lunch one day this week!

November 5 – National Donut Day – grab a donut and eat breakfast with your child!

November 11 – Veteran's Day – please let us know if you are a veteran or there is a special veteran in your family – we want to honor you!

November 14 – National Teddy Bear Day! Send your child's favorite bear to school for a Teddy Bear Picnic!

November 27 – Family Feast Day! Check with your child's teacher for what to bring – join us for lunch or sign up for dinner!

November 28–29 CLOSED for Thanksgiving and Teacher In-Service

Family Engagement
You Matter to Us!
5th Annual Family Night
November 30, 20**

Permission granted by the Hasselbring family, 2021

Have you reviewed our family engagement policy lately? Do you need a refresher on what we offer to our families?

If you answered either "no" or "yes," then join us on November 30, at 6 p.m. for dinner and a brief overview of the upcoming 20** opportunities to engage with us and the community! After a long day of Black Friday shopping, this will be just the break you need! Take a nap, then join us for a light meal – no TURKEY is on the menu!

After, we will have family games and activities available – stay as long as you'd like! This is one of our favorite ways to get all of our families together to share and learn more about each other!

Family Engagement Coordinator, Ms. Kym, will pass out a short survey of interests and needs along with a packet of our updated policy, procedures, forms you will need for the next school year, and overall general information to refresh and rejuvenate our relationships with you, our treasured families! We are looking for two new mentor families as well!

There will also be some community members from local services and businesses to engage in a roundtable discussion on how we can make our community stronger and better support the education of your children.

This will be an evening of fun and relaxation, with just a touch of "business" included! Can't join us? No worries – see Ms. Kym for your packet or to set up an individual meeting!

Personal collection (McKay, 2021)

Speaking of Ms. Kym!!!

Join me in celebrating Ms. Kym, our awesome Pre-K teacher and Family Engagement Coordinator as our Educator of the Month! Ms. Kym has been with our program since 1995 and has contributed to the success of hundreds of Pre-Ks in her lengthy career! As a lifelong learner, we also applaud her recent graduation and earning her bachelor's in ECE! We will be celebrating all month – but will have a special recognition from 4–6 in the family resource room. Please join us for cake and beverages!

Remember to Check Your Child's Classroom Notes!

Celebrations Calendar
January Celebrations

1 New Year's Day	2 National Bath Safety Month	3 Fruitcake Toss Day	4 National Spaghetti Day	5 Bird Day	6 National Cuddle Day	7 Old Rock Day
8 Bubble Bath Day	9 National Soup Month	10 National Letter Writing Week	11 Learn Your Name in Morse Code Day	12 Hot Tea Day	13 Rubber Ducky Day	14 Dress Up Your Pet Day
15 National Hat Day	16 National Nothing Day	17 Ditch Your New Year's Resolution Day	18 Winnie-the-Pooh Day	19 Popcorn Day	20 National Cheese Lover's Day	21 Hugging Day
22 Blonde Brownie Day	23 National Pie Day	24 Belly Laugh Day	25 National Bubble Wrap Day	26 National Oatmeal Month	27 Chocolate Cake Day	28 National Kazoo Day
29 National Puzzle Day	30 National Seed Swap Day	31 Inspire Your Heart with Art Day				

Appendix D
Sample Parent Handbook Outline to Include Family Engagement Policy

A. Introduction
B. Vision Statement
C. Mission Statement
D. Relationship Building
   a. Parent Tours and Information
   b. Welcome/Reception Area
   c. Parking
   d. Family Resource Room
   e. Home Visits
   f. Intake Survey
E. Communications
   a. Communication Preference Form
   b. Family Surveys
   c. Smart phone app
   d. Facebook (Social Media) and/or Website
   e. Family Resource Room
   f. Home Visits
F. Learning at Home and in Community
   a. Child Development and Parenting Classes
   b. Take-Home Activity Bags
   c. Community Events

G. Supporting Educational Progress
   a. Curriculum Overview
   b. Developmental Milestones
   c. State Early Learning Guidelines
   d. Parent Conferences
H. Program Engagement
   a. Family Advisory Council
   b. Family Mentor Program

Appendix E
Sample Practitioner Handbook Outline to Include Family Engagement Policy

I. Introduction
II. Vision Statement
III. Mission Statement
IV. Relationship Building
   a. Classroom Information
   b. Family Resource Bulletin Board
   c. Home Visits
   d. Family Interests/Talents Survey
V. Communications
   a. Communication Preference Form
   b. Communication Tracking Form
   c. Daily Information Sheets
   d. Smart phone app
   e. Blogs
VI. Learning at Home and in Community
   a. Child Development Articles
   b. Classroom Newsletter
   c. Take-Home Activity Bags
   d. Community Events

VII. Supporting Educational Progress
   a. Curriculum Overview
   b. Developmental Milestones
   c. State Early Learning Guidelines
   d. Parent Conferences
       i. Family Questionnaires (ASQ for example)
       ii. Family Goals Sheet
VIII. Program Engagement
   a. Family Advisory Council
   b. Family Mentor Program

Appendix F
Family Engagement Plan Template

ABC Child Development Center's Family Engagement Policy

I. **Introduction**
II. **Our Vision**
III. **Our Mission**
IV. **Program/Family Relationships**
    a. Why are relationships important in your program?
    b. Who is involved in the relationship building?
    c. What will the relationships involve?
    d. Where will the relationships be formed?
    e. When will there be opportunities for the relationships to be formed?
    f. How will they be formed?
V. **Communication Forms and Strategies**
    a. Why is communication important in your program?
    b. Who will be involved in the communications?
    c. What forms will be used? What information will be shared?
    d. Where will the communications be given, located?
    e. When will communications occur?
    f. How will they be given?
VI. **Learning Opportunities at Home**
    a. Why is your program providing these opportunities?
    b. Who will provide these activities?

Appendix F

    c. What forms will they be presented in?
    d. Where will they be provided?
    e. When will they be presented?
    f. How will they be provided?

VII. Learning Opportunities in the Community
    a. Why are community opportunities important to families?
    b. Who will be involved in these opportunities?
    c. What opportunities will be shared?
    d. Where will they take place?
    e. When will they occur?
    f. How will the program participate? How will families participate?

VIII. Making Decisions and Goals Together
    a. Why is this process important for families and the program?
    b. Who will be involved?
    c. What decisions and goals will be reviewed?
    d. Where will this process occur?
    e. When will it occur?
    f. How will the process work?

IX. Program Engagement Opportunities
    a. Why should families be involved in program engagement?
    b. Who should be involved?
    c. What will it require from the family?
    d. Where will the opportunities take place?
    e. When will the opportunities occur?
    f. How will the family's participation help?

For Product Safety Concerns and Information please contact our EU representative GPSR@taylorandfrancis.com
Taylor & Francis Verlag GmbH, Kaufingerstraße 24, 80331 München, Germany

www.ingramcontent.com/pod-product-compliance
Lightning Source LLC
Chambersburg PA
CBHW061843300426
44115CB00013B/2490